PROUST'S DEADLINE

CHRISTINE M. CANO

Proust's Deadline

UNIVERSITY OF ILLINOIS PRESS

URBANA AND CHICAGO

The University of Illinois Press gratefully acknowledges
the support of the W. P. Jones Presidential Faculty
Development Fund in the publication of this volume.

Library of Congress Cataloging-in-Publication Data

Cano, Christine M., 1962–
Proust's deadline / Christine M. Cano.
p. cm.
Includes bibliographical references and index.
ISBN-13: 978-0-252-03070-3 (cloth : alk. paper)
ISBN-10: 0-252-03070-2 (cloth : alk. paper)
1. Proust, Marcel, 1871–1922. A la recherche
du temps perdu.   I. Title.
PQ2631.R63A77387   2006
843'.912—DC22   2006015294

In fond memory of
Anthony R. Pugh
(1931–2004)

Contents

Acknowledgments

I would like to thank Martine Gantrel of Smith College and Michel Raimond of the Sorbonne, whose inspiring teaching sparked in me long ago a deep and lasting interest in Proust. Peter Brooks, who directed my doctoral dissertation on Proust at Yale University, has remained a critical source of guidance ever since. Ora Avni, Susan Blood, and Ben Semple provided invaluable advice on an earlier version of this project. I am especially grateful to Lynne Huffer, who led me to envisage the theoretical framework of this book in new ways.

A number of people and institutions have been of direct assistance in the completion of *Proust's Deadline.* In the fall of 2002, a generous grant from the W. P. Jones Presidential Faculty Development Fund supported archival research at the Bibliothèque Nationale de France. I am indebted to the University of Illinois Press, and especially to its director, Willis Regier. His dedication, enthusiasm, and sense of humor have made the final stages of book production a delight. Armine Kotin Mortimer gave the entire manuscript a careful reading and offered excellent suggestions for revision. James Austin, Sam Bloom, and Sharon Johnson have taken the time to read key sections of the manuscript along the way. Colleagues Gerd Bayer, Georgia Cowart, Beate Diehl, Kurt Koenigsberger, Yuxiu Liang, and Bill Siebenschuh have been extremely helpful as readers and as sources of encouragement. My grandmother, Solveig Pederson, and my parents, Janice K. and

Narciso P. Cano, deserve special recognition for their loving support throughout the writing process. Finally, Janice H. Kaufman's
generous loan of her house and office in Oneonta, New York, in
the summer of 2004, allowed me to finish the book in the peace of
the Catskills.

At Case Western Reserve University, it has been my good for-
tune to have Alan Rocke as a mentor and Mary E. Davis as a friend
and interlocutor. I wish to express my heartfelt gratitude to both
for seeing me through this project from start to finish.

Part of the fourth chapter of *Proust's Deadline* appeared, in a
somewhat different form, as "Death as Editor," in *Proust in Perspective: Visions and Revisions,* ed. Katherine Kolb and Armine
Kotin Mortimer (Urbana and Chicago: University of Illinois Press,
2002), 45–56. I thank the Press for allowing me to reprint the
material here.

This book is dedicated to the memory of Anthony R. Pugh,
devoted Proust scholar and extraordinary friend.

A Note on Quotations

Quotations from Proust's letters are taken from Philip Kolb's twenty-one-volume edition of the *Correspondance* (referenced as *Corr.*, followed by volume and page numbers)—with the exception of a handful of letters to Gaston Gallimard not included in the *Correspondance*. In those instances, I have quoted from Pascal Fouché's edition of Proust's correspondence with Gallimard. English translations, when followed by volume and page numbers, are from Kolb's four-volume *Selected Letters* (translated by Terence Kilmartin, Joanna Kilmartin, and Ralph Manheim; referenced as *SL*). When quoting from *À la recherche du temps perdu*, I cite the four-volume Pléiade edition directed by Jean-Yves Tadié (referenced as *RTP*, followed by volume and page numbers). I then quote from Terence Kilmartin and Andreas Mayor's revision of C. K. Scott Moncrieff's three-volume *Remembrance of Things Past*—the English translation most likely to be found in university libraries.

All translations of French sources not followed by a page number are my own. On occasion, I have taken the liberty of translating very brief phrases from the French directly into English, without citing the original, for the sake of simplicity.

PROUST'S DEADLINE

Introduction

"Life is too short and Proust is too long":[1] Anatole France's wry remark has long made the rounds as a humorous summing-up, and an implicit casting-off, of one of the most important and most difficult literary works of the twentieth century, the 3,000-page *À la recherche du temps perdu*. France's sharp assessment, whose repetition is always greeted with delight, reveals something about the famous readerly ambivalence that haunts Proust's novel even as its canonical status grows ever more secure. What it reveals is the extent to which all reading, but perhaps paradigmatically the reading of Proust, is defined by an extra-textual temporality that is quite simply the time a text "takes" to read—time taken away, France implies, from living itself. *Life is too short:* this banal adage inscribes every reader's mortality into the project of reading Proust, conjuring up an image of the page-turning reader's lifeblood seeping away as she makes her way to the end of yet another complex Proustian sentence. *Proust is too long:* now almost an axiom itself, this tautological formula seems either to sanction the blithe abandonment of our reading efforts, or to call for a remedy to the excess—abridgment, condensation, omitting a volume here and there.[2] Either way, the brevity of life and the length of Proust remain fatally pitted against one another, underscoring the inevitable implication of actual lived temporality in the reading process.

I begin with Anatole France's pithy gloss on reading Proust because I want to make the point that Proust knew it better than any of us. That life was too short—too short, he feared, to complete his writing project, too short to finish correcting his proofs, too short to see the next volume through the publication process; and that his novel was too long—too long for the current book market, too long to be held in the reader's mind over several volumes, too long especially to be grasped all at one go. Although Proust's writing process was accompanied from the start by a sense that time was running out, it was principally through the publication process that he was confronted with the pragmatic and theoretical problem of his novel's extraordinary length. Pragmatic, because in 1912 the average length of books published by the Nouvelle Revue Française, his preferred publisher, was 230 pages (Assouline, *Gaston Gallimard,* 59); theoretical, because the necessity of fragmenting the work into successive volumes introduced into the reading experience a duration, and a set of intervals, foreign to the temporality at play in the text itself.[3] The scope of that duration is dramatic: Proust's multivolume novel was published over a period of fourteen years, from 1913 (*Du côté de chez Swann*) to 1927 (*Le Temps retrouvé,* the last of three posthumous volumes). Much of that period was concomitant with the writing process itself, which arguably spanned the years between 1908 and Proust's death in 1922.

Proust's Deadline is concerned with the temporality of the writing and publishing processes (and, by implication, that of the reading process), especially as Proust articulated it in his correspondence with publishers, potential readers, and critics. Although much attention has been given to Proust's celebrated reflections on the redemption of time through aesthetic form—staged in the pages of *Le Temps retrouvé* as the hero-narrator's discovery of his literary vocation—another significant construction of temporality emerges from Proust's correspondence, less decidedly triumphant in its articulations. This extratextual construction of temporality unfolds largely as a preoccupation with the duration of an extended creative process, a duration conceived by Proust as a constant threat to the putative unity of his meticulously constructed œuvre. His repeated insistence on the "rigorous" structure of the *Recherche* appears in this context as a symbolic effort to guard the work's integrity against the eventual discontinuities of passing time: an incomplete or fragmented publication, an interrupted reading process, a premature death.

Offered as a contribution to our understanding of Proustian temporality, *Proust's Deadline* also means to intervene in a long-standing critical discussion of metaphor and metonymy in relationship to *À la recherche du temps perdu*. Metaphor and metonymy, the focus of a series of now canonical critical readings of the *Recherche*, have been consecrated as key modes for apprehending both the rhetorical tissue of Proust's novel and the functioning of the text as a whole. From Leo Spitzer's 1961 study of Proust's style to Paul de Man's landmark analysis in *Allegories of Reading* and beyond, metaphor has long been promoted as the dominant figure of Proustian expression (notwithstanding de Man's familiar conclusion that metaphor in Proust actually functions as a kind of metonymy; see de Man, "Reading (Proust)"). Often invoked as textual support for this critical privileging of metaphor is a significant passage from *Le Temps retrouvé* where Proust's narrator posits metaphor as a foundational trope for the entire writing project, trumpeting the fixture of the past in the "necessary rings" of metaphor as a victory over contingency—the redemption of experience from the annihilating flight of time.[4]

I recall this critical focus on metaphor and metonymy because it captures much of what is at stake in my discussion of extratextual temporality. Metaphor, the figure of necessity, has come to be identified with the totalization offered by aesthetic form; metonymy, the figure of contingency, connotes fragmentation and rupture. As the vehicles of an opposition based largely on totality and fragmentariness, metaphor and metonymy—in parallel with the Romantic opposition between symbol and allegory—present fundamental ways of thinking about the structure and coherence of literary works. (In his well-known essay "The Metaphoric and Metonymic Poles," Roman Jakobson characterizes as "metaphoric" and "metonymic" entire modes of thought. "The development of a discourse may take place along two different semantic lines: one topic may lead to another either through their similarity or through their contiguity. The metaphoric way would be the most appropriate term for the first case and the metonymic way for the second, since they find their most condensed expression in metaphor and metonymy respectively" [*Fundamentals of Language*, 76]). The claims made by Proust's narrator in favor of the redemptive power of metaphor, often considered to be at the heart of the aesthetic doctrine developed in *Le Temps retrouvé*, are also at work outside the text, and most markedly in the context of Proust's encounter with the publication process. But whereas the novel ends on the apparent triumph of such claims, I suggest here that it is a metonymical mode that dominates Proust's conception and representations of his writing experience. His repeated use of metaphor to assert the preliminary unity of the *Recherche*, and later to convey what he thought of as its impeccable coherence, should be understood in the context of his preoccupation with the threat of fragmentation and discontinuity—possibilities that he evoked most frequently in two guises, editorial intervention and death. In short, *Proust's Deadline* can be inscribed among a number of critical studies that have asserted, following de Man, that the text's primary mode is metonymical or allegorical;[5] but I reach my conclusions through readings of extratextual materials concerning the production, the publication, and the reception history of Proust's novel.

The tension between wholeness and fragmentation implied in the historical oppositions of organic theory—symbol versus allegory, metaphor versus metonymy—runs through Proust's correspondence like a leitmotif during the last thirteen-odd years of his life.[6] I focus on the correspondence in the first two chapters of this book because it serves as a passageway between Proust's formal and theoretical considerations during the writing process and his representation of his work for the public eye. It is in his correspondence that Proust begins to announce a work-in-progress to prospective readers, sketching out the shape of the book to come long before all is written—much as his publishers Grasset and Gallimard will later announce future volumes of the *Recherche*, as phantasmatic projections that create engagement and suspense but do not guarantee production. It is also in his correspondence that Proust begins to formulate a literary strategy for the marketing of his book, preparing it for its transformation into an object of public consumption (in the palpable anxiety of relinquishing control over the reading process once it passes into the public realm).

Chapter 1, "Forthcoming," treats Proust's announcements of the work to come and his articulation of a literary strategy as expressions of a consistent effort to maintain the symbolic coherence of the whole over the indeterminate duration of the writing and publication processes. It opens with a reading of one of Proust's earliest and most famous expressions of that symbolic coherence: a 1909 letter to Geneviève Straus in which he first suggests that the beginning and end of his novel were simultaneously conceived and drafted in tandem. Let me add that although I evoke Proust's narrative of the genesis of his novel, my approach to the correspondence is not that of a genetician. I am interested, rather, in representations and symbolic constructs that become apparent as Proust is called upon to define the structural unity and the import of his project to his correspondents—privileged readers, publishers, reviewers.

These constructs reflect a certain notion of organic form that receives its fullest articulation in classical aesthetic theory. Chapter 2, "The Dream of Simultaneous Publication," is supported by this concept of organic form, a concept that calls for contextualization and further definition. Although a number of different ideas are often roped together under the name of organicism, Proust's formulations of the *Recherche* as an indivisible whole governed by an immanent logic specifically echo two basic tenets of organic theory: the idea that an internal purposiveness or finality regulates the "growth" of the work of art from within; and the theoretical suppression of difference between conception and execution, between the idea expressed and its outward form. ("Internal purposiveness" is Immanuel Kant's reformulation of Aristotle's concept of immanent logic [*Poetics,* Chapters 7–10]. As Murray Krieger suggested in *A Reopening of Closure,* the idea of an internal purposiveness explains the organicist elevation of symbol over allegory, since the valorization of symbol is "the elevation of the internally self-sufficient over the dependence on external entities" [6]). At the heart of Proust's claims to have constructed an indivisible whole are the temporal concerns of organic theory that were fundamental to nineteenth-century organicism.[7]

The framework I adopt in Chapter 2 offers a precise enunciation of these temporal problems through the writings of Gabriel Séailles, whose 1883 treatise *Le Génie dans l'art* best represents the brand of vitalistic organicism that dominated late nineteenth-century French thinking on creative process.

Substantial critical attention has been given to establishing Proust's intellectual debt to the transcendental idealism that Séailles and his cohort reformulated and disseminated in France around the turn of the century.[8] Proust was personally acquainted with Séailles's theories, having attended his aesthetics course at the Sorbonne in 1894–95, but this is of secondary interest to me here. Rather than contribute to the further establishment of Proust's nineteenth-century intellectual heritage, I wish to bring to light a certain theoretical problem that figures prominently in the work of Séailles and that was central to Proust's articulation of his writing experience. The temporal, developmental understanding of organicism characteristic of the nineteenth century, which subtends all of Séailles's writing, is most powerfully condensed in his insistence that the artist must create the illusion of a simultaneously executed whole. Séailles's elaboration of the problem posed by creative process itself, that is, by the *successivity* of process, lends perfect expression to the lived drama of *À la recherche du temps perdu* sketched out by Proust's correspondence: the challenge of conceptualizing and maintaining the text's fundamental identity to itself throughout a lengthy and discontinuous production. Proust's grappling with this theoretical problem took a concrete, narratable form in his prescriptions and specifications to publishers. Understood as the question of real time inscribed in the literary work as difference and rupture, it has also been a recurrent theme of Proust criticism—notably with respect to two major contingencies that arose during the fourteen-year span of the writing process.

Chapters 3 and 4 address these two contingencies—test cases, in a sense, of Proust's assertions that his novel was conceived in such a way as to withstand the eventualities of passing time. The first, the outbreak of the First World War in August 1914, suspended publication of the *Recherche* from 1914 to 1918 and led to its complete transformation; the second, Proust's death in 1922 while apparently engaged in an extreme revision of the final volumes, may have left the end of the novel in pieces. I treat these two events from the perspective of their reception and interpretation in critical and editorial accounts. Chapter 3, "Organicism Gone Awry," traces the important legacy of one such account in Proust criticism: beginning in the 1930s, Proust's earliest genetic critics construed his wartime revisions as a kind of traumatic rupture from which the text (allegedly intact before the war) never recovered. Their portrayal of the postwar version as structurally monstrous was linked to Proust's belated development of his heroine Albertine, who first appeared in drafts in 1913, long after he began writing.[9] Significantly, one of these studies set off decades of critical controversy by tracing Albertine's extratextual origins directly to a biographical episode revolving around a male love object. Her ambiguous status as textual creation and as a possible conduit between life and fiction has been a source of fascination for critics ever since. Albertine's genesis, represented as an unforeseen disturbance in a previously coherent fictional whole or, on the contrary, as the very guarantee of the continuity and coherence of the *Recherche,* has become an important topos for considering interruption and accident in the writing process—possibilities that haunted Proust from the start.

Chapter 4, "Grasset's Revenge," treats an ongoing polemic that the French daily *Libération* once dubbed "the war of the Prousts" (May 2, 1991, 20). The chapter's title refers to the 1987 publication of *Albertine disparue* by Grasset Editions—Grasset's revenge, as one critic has suggested, for losing Proust to Gallimard back in 1916 (McDonald, *The Proustian Fabric,* 10). The war years had given Proust an occasion to break his contract with Grasset and sign on with Gallimard, long his publisher of choice; Gallimard then remained Proust's exclusive publisher until the last of his manuscripts entered the public domain in 1987.[10] Grasset's *Albertine disparue,* whose publication happened to coincide with the end of Gallimard's seventy-year monopoly, was unique among the many new editions that appeared after 1987. It was based on an unpublished typescript revised by Proust just before his death and rediscovered among a relative's belongings; it differed dramatically from previous editions of the same volume (*Albertine disparue* or *La Fugitive*), omitting some 250 pages; and, most important, it was the only new edition to put into question the ideology of Gallimard Editions, which had presented *À la recherche du temps perdu* as a completed work ever since Proust's death.

The resistance to Grasset's *Albertine disparue* was swift and multifaceted. Proust's deathbed revisions to the penultimate volume of the *Recherche* seemed to demolish the coherence of the novel's end in view of a larger, unknown, and unaccomplished plan (possibly the addition of several more volumes). The arguments that took shape against its inclusion in the *Recherche* came from different quarters but shared a basic refusal to sacrifice the narrative and morphological wholeness of the text—whatever the precise evidence given for rejecting the Grasset edition's claims to exclusive authority. Many, though not all, of these arguments were advanced by the editors of new, post–public domain editions of *Albertine disparue* in support of their particular editorial philosophy. From the reader's point of view, the war of the Prousts has meant choosing between these competing editions—choosing, in some cases, between the satisfaction of a coherent ending and the brutal splintering of the end by Proust's untimely death.

The literary *querelle* incited by Grasset's *Albertine disparue* played out its initial round in three types of venues: scholarly journals, the French and Italian press, and the paratext of each new edition of the volume. These materials serve as my main texts for Chapter 4. My point is not to rehearse the hypotheses that have sustained this debate, but to lend them a wider context as they map out the most recent, and for some the most traumatic, episode in a publication history that began precisely with Proust's refusal to fragment a text that he considered to be an indivisible whole.[11] In so doing, I also propose that Proust's revisions to *Albertine disparue* can be read within the context of his own definitions of narrative coherence and artificial closure, concepts that unfolded throughout the publication of *Du côté de chez Swann*.

The final, or at least the most recent, peripeteia in the story of the *Recherche*—the loss of a stable, basic text—has brought to the fore the very preoccupations that defined Proust's writing project from the beginning. Proust's repeated assertions of preliminary unity and completion, and his long resistance to fragmentation, were precautions taken against the eventual assaults of time on the fragile process of transmitting meaning through writing. I associated these preoccupations earlier with the opposition between metaphor and metonymy. It seems fitting that Albertine, classically defined as an element of raw life (thus contingent, metonymic) disrupting an autonomous, fictional whole (metaphoric), should now be the vehicle of what appears to be the text's metonymic undoing by time. The tale of that undoing, told in the following pages, underscores the sinister implications of all writing practices, implications of which Proust was radically aware. Writing is the horizontal line that marks the passage of time and is *itself* the passage of time, a linear displacement leading toward death. Read as an appeal to the power of poetic language to overcome contingency, *À la recherche du temps perdu* may be all the more eloquent because of it.

1 *Forthcoming: Announcing the* Recherche

> Vous le comprendrez facilement, je travaille depuis longtemps à cette œuvre, j'y ai mis le meilleur de ma pensée; elle réclame maintenant un tombeau qui soit achevé avant que le mien soit rempli.
>
> You will readily understand: I've been working on this book for a long time and have put the best of myself into it; now it is clamoring for a tomb that can be completed before my own is filled.
>
> —Proust to René Blum, February 1913[1]

Like most novels published in France at the beginning of the twentieth century, *À la recherche du temps perdu* was the object of a strategic publicity campaign designed to hook the interest of readers even before the book appeared. Commissioned book reviews in the French press, excerpts published in prominent literary journals, announcements of volumes to come: these appeals to a prospective or continuing readership preceded, and then accompanied, the publication of each installment of Proust's multivolume novel—from the appearance of *Du côté de chez Swann* in 1913 to the staccato publication of volumes throughout the 1920s, several of them posthumous. But long before the novel's first volume saw the light of day, it was Proust himself who initiated the process by announcing to his correspondents, often tentatively and with very little written, his literary plans. A series of such advertisements announcing the book to come punctuates Proust's correspondence over many years, publicly engaging him to the undertaking of a project and to its eventual completion. Of these announcements, one in particular, a 1909 letter sent from a seaside resort, has acquired a significant symbolic charge for critics.

Writing from Cabourg, Normandy, in August 1909, Proust announced in a letter to his longtime friend Geneviève Straus that he had just begun—and finished—a whole long book. "Vous me lirez—," he wrote, "et plus que vous ne voudrez—car je viens de commencer—et de finir—tout un long livre" (You will read me—more of me than you will want—for I've just begun—and finished—a whole long book) (*Corr.*, 9:163; *SL*, 2:445–46). Perhaps the most frequently quoted passage in all of Proust's correspondence, these words have become identified with the genesis of *À la recherche du temps perdu*. Classically interpreted as recording an epiphany and a turning point in Proust's writing process, the letter to Madame Straus allegedly marks the frontier between his original project for a critical essay, *Contre Sainte-Beuve*, and the start of the *Recherche*—that is, the frontier between theory and fiction.[2] The seemingly immediate expression "I have just begun—and finished" has come to symbolize Proust's discovery of a structure for his future novel, a structure based on the articulation between beginning and end. In reality, "to begin" and "to finish" condense months of writing into a single laconic phrase, and the breakthrough that allowed Proust to move from essay to novel—so often characterized as a spontaneous "illumination"—has also been construed as a series of decisive moments spread out over several years.[3]

But whether or not Proust's 1909 announcement of his future book marks an epiphany, it is in this passage that he first set forth the terms in which he would continually define and defend what he called the "construction" of *À la recherche du temps perdu*.[4] For years to come, Proust invoked the near-simultaneous composition of the novel's beginning and end whenever its coherence came under attack—and especially in 1919–20, when critics responded to the publication of *À l'Ombre des jeunes filles en fleurs*. Reacting to a December 12, 1919, review by Jean de Pierrefeu in the *Journal des Débats*, Proust wrote to critic André

Chaumeix that the last chapter had actually been written *before* the first. "Si vous avez quelquefois l'occasion de causer avec Monsieur de Pierrefeu, vous pourrez lui dire que le dernier chapitre de mon œuvre ayant été écrit avant le premier, et tout l'ouvrage étant fait et terminé, il n'a pas besoin d'attendre ma mort, comme il dit, pour voir finir *À la recherche du temps perdu*" (If ever you have the chance to chat with Monsieur de Pierrefeu, do tell him that since the last chapter of my novel was written before the first, and since the entire work is done and finished, he needn't wait for my death, as he says, to see the end of *À la recherche du temps perdu*) (*Corr.*, 18:524). And a few days later, in a famous response to Paul Souday of *Le Temps*, Proust reasserted the meticulous construction of the whole in a formula that has become the emblem of that construction. "Le dernier chapitre du dernier volume a été écrit tout de suite après le premier chapitre du premier volume. Tout l'"entre-deux' a été écrit ensuite" (The last chapter of the last volume was written immediately after the first chapter of the first volume. The entire "in-between" was written next) (*Corr.*, 18:536). Before, immediately after: small variations in a formula repeatedly presented as compelling evidence of the rigorous structure of the *Recherche.*

The 1909 letter to Madame Straus continues: "Mais je voudrais bien finir, aboutir. Si tout est écrit, beaucoup de choses sont à remanier" (But I'd love to finish, get to the end of it. If everything is written, a lot of things have yet to be revised) (*Corr.*, 9:163). "Everything is written": Proust's striking assertion of wholeness and completion at the threshold of a writing project that will span thirteen more years—the rest of his life—is hardly to be taken literally. His figurative use of the word *tout* (everything) to designate a text composed of only beginning and end marks the first of his efforts to establish a totalizing metaphor for his *œuvre*, a metaphor that would guard it symbolically against the effects of future discontinuity (that is, against the effects of time itself). From the outset, Proust's representations of his writing process are characterized at once by an insistence on preliminary unity and by an acute consciousness of the eventuality of interruption. The external contingencies that he evoked endlessly in his letters—the possibility of fragmentation or interruption during the publication process, his readers' failure to read through to the end, his own death—function as the counterpart to Proust's unifying metaphor for the text. The metaphorical *tout*, by means of which Proust alleges a simultaneously conceived whole, can be thought of as his initial provision against the pulverizing temporality of writing, publishing, and reading.

Contingencies

Proust's tentative announcements of intention to write were echoed, throughout the editorial history of the *Recherche*, by actual announcements of future volumes that stand behind as curious indices of unfulfilled intentions, changes in plan. When Bernard Grasset published *Du côté de chez Swann* in November 1913, he announced on its flyleaf the upcoming publication of the two volumes meant to complete the tripartite book: "Coming in 1914: *Le Côté de Guermantes. Le Temps retrouvé.*" (The announcement obviously had a provisional nature in Proust's eyes, since he wrote to René Blum, secretary of the prominent newspaper *Le Gil Blas*, that although the titles of the next volumes had already been announced, he might call the second volume *À l'Ombre des jeunes filles en fleurs* or *Les Intermittences du cœur* or *L'Adoration perpétuelle* or *Les Colombes poignardées* [*Corr.*, 12:295].) The volumes named in the advertisement would not appear in 1914, and they would never appear as such. August 1914 saw the outbreak of war, Bernard Grasset's mobilization, and the reduction of activity at Grasset Editions to a minimum; the publication of the *Recherche* was suspended indefinitely as the publishing house all but closed. The second volume announced had been set into proofs (the famous Grasset *placards*), while the third and final volume was in an indeterminate state of composition.[5] These two projected volumes later became the object of much critical speculation, of attempted reconstructions, and even of a certain nostalgia for an "original," compact version of the *Recherche*—Proust's novel as it might have read before expanding to its gigantic postwar proportions.

Grasset's 1913 promise of volumes to come was revised and displaced by a second announcement made some five years later (November 1918) and by a different publisher: Gallimard Editions.[6] On the back cover of the novel's new second volume, *À l'Ombre des jeunes filles en fleurs*, the three volumes projected in 1913 had metamorphosed into five. *Le Côté de Guermantes*, originally announced as the second volume, had been displaced by *À l'Ombre des jeunes filles en fleurs* and its publication pushed even farther into the future under the heading "In press," with no date specified. *Le Temps retrouvé*, originally the third volume, had given way to two new volumes, also indicated as being in press: *Sodome et Gomorrhe I* and *Sodome et Gomorrhe II—Le Temps retrouvé*. By the middle of 1920, Gaston Gallimard made yet a new announcement at Proust's behest. "Je crois qu'au revers de l'exemplaire de *Guermantes I*," Proust wrote to Gallimard, "vous devriez annoncer: Pour paraître en décembre [1920], *Guermantes II, Sodome et Gomorrhe I*" (I think you should announce on the back cover of *Guermantes I:* Coming in December [1920], *Guermantes II, Sodome et Gomorrhe I*) (*Corr.*, 19:325). But *Le Côté de Guermantes II* would appear only in April 1921, with the announcement of four future volumes: three more volumes of *Sodome et Gomorrhe* and *Le Temps retrouvé*.

The series was completed by a barely posthumous advertisement that appeared as an insert in the December 1, 1922, issue of *La Nouvelle Revue Française*, some two weeks after Marcel Proust's death (November 18).[7] The advertisement, printed before his death, recapitulates the volumes of *À la recherche du temps perdu* already published by the Nouvelle Revue Française and announces under the rubric "In press": *Sodome et Gomorrhe III—La Prisonnière; Albertine disparue*. These two volumes would appear in 1923 and 1925, respectively. Under a second rubric, "Forthcoming," the uncanny announcement of future volumes that would never materialize: *Sodome et Gomorrhe* in several volumes (*suite*); *Le Temps retrouvé* (conclusion). Although the Nouvelle Revue Française did eventually publish Proust's unrevised notebooks as *Le Temps retrouvé* in 1927, the "sequel" to *Sodome et Gomorrhe* announced here, volumes qualified by an indefinite "several," was pure projection in December 1922. The advertisement would not be an unfitting epitaph for Proust, who in the final years of his life had come to identify himself entirely with his *œuvre:* pointing toward the future of a *Recherche* that is always already finished, the posthumous announcement represents both preliminary closure and endless expansion. It fixes in print, as unrealized potential, the characteristic forward movement of *À la recherche du temps perdu*, the perpetual swell of the in-between flanked by an immutable beginning and end.

These editorial announcements trace an itinerary distinct from the published text of *À la recherche du temps perdu* as we have come to know it. Read as an ensemble, they form not a coherent succession of volumes but rather a series of revisions where each projection of the finished whole yields to the next. Created as part of a commercial strategy, they appear in retrospect as the locus of a tension between preliminary intentions and projections on the one hand, the contingencies of the writing process on the other. Such contingencies were typically articulated by Proust as matters of life and death. In a paradigmatic 1921 letter to Gaston Gallimard, Proust evoked four future volumes of the *Recherche* with a parenthetical caution: "*Sodome II, Sodome III, Sodome IV* et *Le Temps retrouvé*, quatre longs volumes qui se succéderont à intervalles assez espacés (si Dieu me prête vie)" (four long volumes to follow at fairly long intervals [if God grants me life], *Sodome II, Sodome III, Sodome IV* and *Le Temps retrouvé*) (*Corr.*, 20:53; *SL*, 4:186). The inevitable link that asserts itself between future volumes and an impending death suggests that the specter of a premature end has a structural function in the writing process. The standard caveat that follows Proust's announcements that he has begun to write functions less as a caution than as a wager:[8] it provides an agonistic structure where (the idea of) death serves as a constant threat to the work's completion and organizes it negatively. Questions of length, format, division into volumes, intervals between volumes, and dates of publication all become crucial in their contingency, as references to an imminent death eventually enter into every aspect of editorial production.

From 1909 until his death in 1922, Proust's correspondence is dominated by two paradoxical concerns: that *something* of his writing project, some part of it, reach the public realm before his death; and that the integrity of the work be maintained throughout the publishing process—that it remain a single work, an undivided whole (symbolically, if not materially). In one of his earliest provisions for his eventual death, Proust envisioned the separate publication of an early version of "Combray," the first part of *Du côté de chez Swann,* suggesting that it could represent the whole if the publication process went no farther. Seeking a publisher for what he then called simply *Sainte-Beuve,* he addressed this request to his friend Georges de Lauris in December 1909: "Je voulais vous écrire pour vous demander . . . si vous pensiez que si je disparaissais en ce moment sans plus lointain achèvement du livre, cette partie est publiable en volume et si, dans ce cas vous voudriez, le cas échéant, y veiller" (I wanted to write to you to ask . . . whether you think that if I were to die now without any further completion of the book, this part is publishable as a volume, and whether in that case you would look after it) (*Corr.,* 9:226; *SL,* 2:461). *Du côté de chez Swann* would later retain for Proust the distinction of its relative autonomy with respect to the rest of the novel. But if in 1909 it was possible for him to imagine publication of "Combray" as a separate volume, by 1912 the very idea of division into parts had become problematic. Even the prospect of leaving intervals between the publication of different volumes was troublesome—Proust called it contrary to the "spirit" of the work, that is, its fundamental unity (*Corr.,* 11:76). By 1913, resigned to the necessity of fragmenting the text into volumes, Proust nonetheless continually reinscribed *Swann* within a larger whole, a whole conceived as analogous to Anatole France's four-volume *Histoire contemporaine* or Maurice Barrès's *Roman de l'énergie nationale:* "Le premier volume (mais il vaudrait mieux ne pas dire le premier volume, car je feins qu'il soit à lui seul un petit tout, comme *L'Orme du mail* dans *Histoire contemporaine* ou *Les Déracinés* dans *Le Roman de l'énergie nationale*) s'appelle: *Du côté de chez Swann*" (The first volume [but it might be better not to say the first volume because I'm claiming it's a small whole unto itself, like *l'Orme du mail* in *Histoire contemporaine* or *Les Déracinés* in *Le Roman de l'énergie nationale*] is called: *Du côté de chez Swann*) (*Corr.,* 12:295).[9] Referring to his first volume as "a small whole unto itself," Proust echoed an earlier conception of *Swann* as autonomous; what had changed is that he no longer considered it publishable as an independent text in the event of his death.

By the time *À la recherche du temps perdu* had expanded to its postwar proportions, not only was it unthinkable to Proust that its parts should be complete in themselves, but nothing short of the written text from beginning to end could serve to represent the project as a whole. "Pourvu que tout paraisse de mon vivant ce sera bien," Proust specified in a well-known 1919 letter to Gaston Gallimard, "et s'il en arrivait autrement, j'ai laissé tous mes cahiers numérotés que vous prendriez et je compte alors sur vous pour faire la publication complète" (As long as everything comes out in my lifetime, all will be well, and should it turn out otherwise, I've left all my exercise-books numbered and ready for you, and I count on you to complete publication) (*Corr.*, 18:226; *SL*, 4:76). And just before his death, after correcting the proofs of *La Prisonnière*, Proust repeated himself in a final letter to Gallimard, but with a trace of urgency: "Je crois en ce moment que le plus urgent serait de vous livrer tous mes livres" (I think the most urgent thing now would be to turn over to you every one of my books) (*Corr.*, 21:529). A redefinition had taken place between the two solutions to incompleteness (part for whole, or surrender of all material for posthumous publication): the *Recherche* was no longer communicable as a schematic representation. It had ceased to be reducible either to one of its parts or to any paradigm, including announcements, meant to represent the text independently of its actual production over time.

Severe and Complex

Proust's investment in the indivisibility of the whole became especially apparent in the year preceding the publication of *Du côté de chez Swann*, the first volume of a three-part ensemble that would be advertised as a "trilogy."[10] An ongoing explicative discourse served to explain to his correspondents and potential readers that this first part was inseparable from the others both in form and in meaning, and that its significance would become clear only by the end of the third volume. *Du côté de chez Swann* was a prelude, full of *preparations*—Proust tellingly compared it to a Wagnerian overture whose musical themes, unbeknownst to the listener, were actually leitmotifs that would recur throughout the opera (*Corr.*,

12:265; *SL,* 3:205). The composition of *Swann,* he repeatedly asserted, was at once *severe* and *complex:* in other words, its structure was so perfectly calculated that it contained no idle detail, and yet the function of any detail was necessarily hidden (veiled, as Proust often said) in a reading of the first volume alone. Writing to Louis de Robert in October 1912, Proust suggested that the narrative's complexity might obscure its severity: "J'ai travaillé vous le saurez peut-être depuis que je suis si malade à un long ouvrage que j'appelle roman, parce qu'il n'a pas la contingence de Mémoires . . . et qu'il est d'une composition très sévère, quoique peu saisissable parce que complexe" (I have been working as you may perhaps know, ever since I've been so ill, on a long work which I call a novel because it hasn't the fortuitousness of memoirs . . . and its design is extremely rigorous although not easily grasped because of its complexity) (*Corr.,* 11:251; *SL,* 3:106). Such terms became more frequent as the publication of *Swann* approached. To René Blum, Proust described the novel as "un tout très composé, quoique d'une composition si complexe que je crains que personne ne le perçoive et qu'il apparaisse comme une suite de digressions. C'est tout le contraire" (a carefully composed whole, though so complex in structure that I'm afraid no one will notice it and that it will seem to be a series of digressions. It's exactly the opposite) (*Corr.,* 12:82; *SL,* 3:153 [translation modified]). He specified to Blum a few days later that its composition was "si complexe qu'elle n'apparaît que très tardivement quand tous les 'Thèmes' ont commencé à se combiner" (so complex that it only becomes clear much later when all the "themes" have begun to coalesce) (*Corr.,* 12:92; *SL,* 3:159).

But not only was the comprehension of this first volume to be deferred to later volumes, the narrative was designed to leave the reader mistaken as to the meaning of the whole. "Ce n'est qu'à la fin du livre," Proust explained to Jacques Rivière after the publication of *Swann,* "et une fois les leçons de la vie comprises, que ma pensée se dévoilera. Celle que j'exprime à la fin du premier volume . . . est *le contraire* de ma conclusion" (It's only at the end of the book, when the lessons of life have been grasped, that my design will become clear. The thought I express at the end of the first volume . . . is the *opposite* of my conclusion). He went on to propose an analogy with Wagner's *Parsifal:*

Si on en induisait que ma pensée est un scepticisme désenchanté, ce serait absolument comme si un spectateur ayant vu, à la fin du premier acte de *Parsifal,* ce personnage ne rien comprendre à la cérémonie et être chassé par Gurnemantz [*sic*], supposait que Wagner a voulu dire que la simplicité du cœur ne conduit à rien. Dans ce premier volume vous avez vu le plaisir que me cause la sensation de la madeleine trempée dans le thé, je dis que je cesse de me sentir mortel etc. et que je ne comprends pas pourquoi. Je ne l'expliquerai qu'à la fin du troisième volume. *Tout est ainsi construit (Corr.,* 13:99, italics mine).

If anyone were to infer therefrom that my philosophy is a disenchanted skepticism, it would be just as though an opera-goer, having seen the hero failing to understand the ceremony at the end of the first act of *Parsifal* and being sent packing by Gurnemanz, were to imagine that Wagner meant to show that simplicity of the heart leads nowhere. In this first volume you have seen the pleasurable sensation the madeleine soaked in tea gives me—as I say, I cease to feel mortal etc. and I can't understand why. I'll explain it only at the end of the third volume. *The whole thing is constructed this way (SL,* 3:233).

Two kinds of misreading, then, were likely to occur upon a reading of *Swann:* the text would appear to be lacking in structure ("a series of digressions"), or it would induce to mistaken conclusions. Proust had defined the term *préparer* in precisely this way: to "prepare" future volumes within this first volume was not simply to introduce or announce (themes and characters, for example) but to *mislead.* "Il y a beaucoup de personnages; ils sont 'préparés' dès ce premier volume, c'est-à-dire qu'ils feront dans le second exactement le contraire de ce à quoi on s'attendait d'après le premier" (There are a great many characters; they are "prepared" in this first volume, in such a way that in the second they will do exactly the opposite of what one would have expected from the first) *(Corr.,* 12:92; *SL,* 3:158). And in response to Francis Chevassu's December 7, 1913, review of *Du côté de chez Swann*—in which Chevassu spoke of a whimsical structure and an absence of plot—Proust called the composition of *Swann* "la plus volontaire et la plus calculée" (as deliberate and calculated as possible). His examples of composition are unequivocal: composition is the deferred correction of a first impression. Proust cites the initial presentation of the musician Vinteuil: "J'ai soin dans mon premier chapitre de montrer un vieillard qui dit des choses ridicules dont personne ne se doute même qu'il compose. Dans la deuxième partie une sublime sonate qui joue un grand rôle dans la vie de Swann se trouve être de cet homme qu'on a trouvé d'autant plus ridicule qu'on ne savait pas préalablement qu'il avait du génie. Est-ce que tout cela n'est pas la composition[?]) (I take care in my first chapter to present an old man who says ridiculous things and of whom nobody suspects that he composes music. In the second part, a sublime sonata that plays an enormous role in Swann's life turns out to be by this man, whom everyone found all the more ridiculous because they didn't know he was a genius. Isn't that what composition is?) (*Corr.*, 12:367).

Proust's insistence that comprehension of the whole will be continuously revised by further reading of the parts suggests a defining feature of the organic whole.[11] The way in which *Du côté de chez Swann* is inseparable from the rest has to do with a withholding of meaning that organizes the entire cycle of novels. There is something that Proust deliberately fails to announce: "J'ai trouvé plus probe et plus délicat comme artiste de ne pas laisser voir, de ne pas annoncer que c'était justement à la recherche de la Vérité que je partais" (I thought it more honorable and tactful as an artist not to let it be seen, not to proclaim, that I was setting out precisely in search of the Truth) (*Corr.*, 13:99; *SL*, 3:232). What is withheld is that the narrative, far from being a series of digressions, organizes itself as a positive itinerary, a "search for Truth"; and whatever *is* announced ("prepared") bears the mark of error and is subject to systematic correction later on. Proust repeatedly invoked this pattern of the self-correcting text as a way of justifying the integrity of the whole and persuading readers to continue on—as when he cautioned Georges de Lauris, a propos of an early version of "Combray," "C'est comme cela à cette *date-là*. Le reste du livre corrigera" (That's how it is at *that moment*. The rest of the book will rectify) (*Corr.*, 9:225). However it might be divided up, the *Recherche* remained an indissoluble "seul et même ouvrage" (single and selfsame work).[12]

Throughout the negotiations that led to the publication of *Du côté de chez Swann*, Proust emphasized this point above all: the

Recherche was governed by an immanent logic, and should for that reason be published and read *as a whole*. What appears in Proust's letters to friends as a determining moment in the creative process—the discovery of a unifying principle in the early stages of writing—had now inscribed itself in the actual text as interdependence of the parts. Proust's compensatory discourse, which he disseminated in letters and interviews alike, was meant to advise prospective readers that despite appearances, *Swann* was not autonomous. As he wrote to Lucien Daudet, passages that appeared to be digressions were part of a plan so deliberate that even the chapter headings of succeeding volumes would reflect the material of the first volume (*Corr.*, 12:258–59). Traces of his previous attitude toward *Du côté de chez Swann*—that it could, in the event of his death, stand on its own—were to be found only in the idea that *Swann* should adequately represent his talent, that it should contain as many "samples" of the rest as possible (Fraisse, *Lire*, 89). Louis de Robert, a longtime friend and one of Proust's first readers, wrote of this period that Proust "doutait alors de son destin, et il s'efforçait de donner sa mesure dans ce premier livre. Il rêvait d'y montrer toutes les nuances de son talent" (was unsure of his fate and tried to prove what he was capable of in this first book. He dreamed of displaying in it every nuance of his talent) (*Comment débuta Marcel Proust*, 13).

By the time Grasset was preparing to launch *Du côté de chez Swann* in the fall of 1913, Proust had long since apprehended the impossibility of summarizing or schematizing (what was then) the entire novel. Whereas in the early stages of his search for a publisher he had sent long, explicative letters along with his manuscript—attempting to communicate the nature and scope of the project in its entirety—his attitude toward publication was now simply pragmatic. The desire to obtain a publisher's complete adherence to his project had given way to an imperious effort to reach readers. Once made public, his novel would then be accessible to a *true* reading, a reading of the whole by way of its progressive but sometimes contradictory stages. But here came the paradox: if something was to be published before his death— imminent, as Proust imagined it—then *Du côté de chez Swann* must appear on its own, and as quickly as possible. Proust would have to accomplish for his readers what he had ceased trying to do in his dealings with publishers. He must communicate the import of *À la recherche du temps perdu* in a single readable summary or fragment—a soundbite, as we might say today.

Prepublications

On the eve of the publication of *Du côté de chez Swann*, Proust was confronted with the specifically commercial necessity of presenting his entire work in schematic and fragmented form. *Échos* and *entrefilets* appeared as brief notices in the press, while excerpts of the text itself were given to newspapers and literary journals as *prépublications*. These *échos* or *entrefilets*—consisting of just a few lines, as their names suggest—were commissioned by the publisher or the author, a typical publicity practice since the late nineteenth century. One of the first such notices to appear was a "literary indiscretion" penned by René Blum for *Le Gil Blas*.

In a letter soliciting the announcement from Blum, Proust attempted to communicate in a few words the quintessence of a 1,500-page text that had become virtually impossible to summarize. Two principal concerns come across in the letter. Proust repeatedly insists that his work is not a "collection" of any kind and that Blum should avoid giving this impression. At the same time, he emphasizes the role of involuntary memory as the structuring device of the entire novel, adding that it serves as a support for something "réel, passionné . . . ne méritant plus l'épithète de 'délicat', de 'fin', mais de vivant et de vrai" (real, passionate . . . no longer deserving epithets like "delicate" and "fine," but rather lifelike and true) (*Corr.*, 12:296).[13] The association between these two concerns is not accidental. With the epithets *délicat* and *fin*, Proust is alluding to the reception of his first published work, *Les Plaisirs et les jours*, a collection of short stories and poems marketed as an illustrated luxury book in 1896. He subtly urges Blum to deflect attention from *Les Plaisirs et les jours*, just as in an earlier letter he took care to dissociate the novel from his *Figaro* articles (1903–9) (*Corr.*, 12:82). But if Proust's remarks to Blum reflect above all a desire to lose the stigma of dilettantism attached to his previous publications, his insistence that the book about to appear is not a collection also points to a fundamental defining feature of the *Recherche:* a continuous whole unified by the notion of involuntary memory, it holds together exactly *unlike* a collection. Elsewhere Proust designates this kind of coherence by the term *ouvrage* (work), continually opposing it to the term *recueil* (collection). His assurances to Georges de Lauris just a few months before the appearance of *Swann* are typical: "Et quelle que soit la longueur du volume si mutilé qu'il soit il y en aura assez pour que vous sentiez que c'est un ouvrage, et non un recueil" (Whatever the length of this volume, however mutilated it is, there will be enough of it that you'll be able to tell it's a work and not a collection) (*Corr.,* 12:229).

The result of Proust's efforts to make himself understood in a few paragraphs can be seen in Blum's announcement, which appeared in *Le Gil Blas* on November 9, 1913, under the rubric "Les Lettres" (reproduced in Lhomeau and Coelho, *Marcel Proust,* 263). After citing briefly Proust's translations of Ruskin and his "collection of essays," *Les Plaisirs et les jours,* Blum goes on to announce *Du côté de chez Swann*:

> Dans quelques jours, l'éditeur Bernard Grasset va publier *Du côté de chez Swann,* le premier roman de cet auteur. Nous y retrouverons, développées, affermies, toutes les qualités de subtile analyse qu'a montrées Monsieur Marcel Proust. Cet ouvrage, le premier d'une série qui aura pour titre général *À la recherche du temps perdu,* joint une étude élégante et ironique de quelques milieux mondains à l'évocation de tendres paysages et de souvenirs d'enfance.

> In a few days, publisher Bernard Grasset will release *Du côté de chez Swann,* the author's first novel. In it you will rediscover—enhanced and strengthened—the gifts for subtle analysis that Monsieur Marcel Proust has already shown. This work, the first in a series whose main title will be *À la recherche du temps perdu,* combines an elegant and ironic study of a few aristocratic circles with an evocation of tender landscapes and childhood memories.

Such an announcement was bound to displease Proust in all of its details. Blum begins by evoking Proust's *Figaro* articles, which he qualifies as "quelques pénétrantes et délicates chroniques" (a few penetrating and subtle articles). (Just after the publication of Blum's *écho*, Proust asked Gaston Calmette, director of *Le Figaro*, to suppress all mention of *Les Plaisirs et les jours*, as well as the adjectives *délicat* and *fin*, in any announcement he might publish [*Corr.*, 12:308–9].) In introducing *Du côté de chez Swann*, Blum says nothing of involuntary memory—the "essence" of the work as emphasized in Proust's letter—but speaks instead of "ironic studies," of "subtle analysis." Blum's announcement is one of the first signs, for Proust, of how difficult it will be to overcome his reputation as a superficial author. It also marks an intersection between the commercial necessity of the schematic formula and Proust's continual efforts to communicate, integrally and faithfully, his lengthy text in such a manner that it will be read as he conceives it: as a whole and living work whose parts are fully interdependent. Léon Pierre-Quint, literary critic and friend of Proust, commented on this disparity in his account of the launching of *Du côté de chez Swann*. "Résumer [le] sens général [de ces recherches sur la mémoire involontaire], leur nouveauté et leur importance dans un entrefilet de quelques lignes devenait une impossibilité presque complète" (To summarize in an announcement of a few lines the general meaning [of Proust's discoveries regarding involuntary memory], their novelty and their importance, was becoming an almost total impossibility) (*Stratégie littéraire*, 54).

To summarize the general meaning of the work was now a near impossibility—and a necessity. In order to circulate among readers, the *Recherche* must first pass through any number of distortions as it was advertised. Proust began to make more frequent use of another supplementary practice designed to introduce readers to the principles of the work before it appeared: private readings of excerpts to friends. Such readings had been a part of Proust's literary strategy from the earliest stages of his writing process, and had sometimes functioned as a temporary substitute for publication when the search for a publisher was particularly discouraging. Now that publication was imminent, they served as new attempts to communicate the quintessence of the entire novel by fragment or sample. Even after René Blum's reductive, formulaic *écho* appeared in *Le Gil Blas*, Proust made another bid for Blum's comprehension, inviting him over one evening to read aloud to him from the manuscript of *Swann*. Awaiting judgment of the whole on the basis of an isolated part, Proust placed particular emphasis on the novel's first instance of involuntary memory, the famous scene of the *madeleine*. As Pierre-Quint has pointed out, Blum was in an ideal position to grasp the significance of this key passage, since Proust had introduced him to the work gradually in the course of their conversations (*Stratégie littéraire*, 58).

Both the *écho* and the prepublished excerpt were meant to accomplish something similar to Proust's private conversations with Blum: initiate readers to the novel in its entirety, by introducing them to its ethos and its structure, before they began to read. Proust seemed to anticipate, however, that prepublications would inevitably serve to represent the whole in the eyes of prospective readers and not simply to prepare them for their reading. As he turned more frequently to the excerpt as a publicity measure, he continued to affirm that the *Recherche* was an *ouvrage*, a whole work, and not a collection of separate parts. Excerpts were useful only insofar as they led to an integral reading of the volume—or replaced the volume with an equivalent, as in the case of serialization in the press. Proust had long entertained this last possibility, despite the disadvantages of fragmentation, before finally signing on with Grasset. (In August 1909 he proposed his *Contre Sainte-Beuve* to Alfred Vallette of *Le Mercure de France*, suggesting publication in the form of regular excerpts from October to January. "La partie roman aurait ainsi paru," he added. "Resterait la longue causerie sur Sainte-Beuve, la critique etc. qui ne paraîtrait que dans le volume" [The novel part would thus have appeared. There would remain the long discussion on Sainte-Beuve, the criticism etc. which would appear only in the book version] [*Corr.*, 9:156; *SL*, 2:443]. Proust's unusual proposal thus called for a scission of his project into two forms, one fragmented and the other integral: "the novel part," the narrative minus its theoretical passages, would appear serially, to be followed by publication of the entire text as a volume. After Vallette declined both parts of the proposal, Proust pursued Gaston Calmette's offer to serialize the manuscript in *Le Figaro.* He was disappointed when the installments never materialized.)[14]

Proust's strategy for introducing readers gradually to the massive text by what Luc Fraisse has called "homeopathic doses" was put into effect as early as the spring of 1912, when he began to offer excerpts of *Du côté de chez Swann* to *Le Figaro* (*Lire*, 6). These excerpts—small prose poems, according to Proust—appeared from March to September 1912, under individual titles: "Épines blanches, épines roses" (White thorns, pink thorns), "Rayon de soleil sur le balcon" (Ray of sunlight on the balcony), and "L'Église de village" (The village church). The use of prepublications intensified in November 1913, with substantial fragments appearing in *Le Gil Blas, Le Temps,* and *Les Annales,* at a time when Proust was most concerned about his work's daunting length. Used properly, fragmentation—whether serial or "homeopathic"—could be put into the service of narrative continuity.

Some ten years into the publication process, Proust was still grappling with the danger posed by prepublications: the possibility that the fragment might supplant the whole in the reader's mind. As he prepared excerpts of *Sodome et Gomorrhe II* (1922) for *La Nouvelle Revue Française,* he warned Gaston Gallimard that "ces coupures démolissent un livre, le lecteur croit avoir tout lu dans la *Revue* et se trompe" (these cuts destroy the book, the reader thinks he's read everything in the *Revue* and is mistaken) (*Corr.,* 20:470). "Les coupures" were cuts within the fragments themselves, the adaptation of specific excerpts to the needs of the journal in which they appeared. After choosing a lengthy excerpt from the end of *Sodome et Gomorrhe II,* Proust specified to Gallimard: "Il faudrait des coupures. Je m'y refuse absolument" (We would have to make cuts. I absolutely refuse). He went on to refer to the controversial offer of another journal, *Les Œuvres libres,* to publish significant excerpts of the same volume:

> Vous craignez qu'un extrait aux *Œuvres libres* empêche de lire le livre. Mais au moins le titre étant différent, il y a chances pour que ce soit le contraire. Dans la *Nouvelle Revue Française* en revanche, où le public est mon public, tout le monde comprendra que c'est la suite, et si je faisais des coupures je mutilerais mon œuvre, car personne ne se reporterait au livre (*Corr.,* 20:463).

> You fear that an extract in *Les Œuvres libres* will discourage peo-
> ple from reading the book. But with a different title, there's at
> least a chance that it will be the other way around. In *La Nouvelle
> Revue Française*, however, whose readership is my readership,
> everybody will realize that it's the sequel and if I made cuts, I
> would be mutilating my own work, for nobody will turn to the
> book (*SL*, 4:253–54).

For "his" readers, the fragment would naturally reinscribe itself
within the continuity of the volume, but it must faithfully reproduce the very text of the volume so that there is no gap between
the excerpt and the continuous volume. Proust's hesitation as to
which fragment to publish in *La Nouvelle Revue Française* points
up a second danger inherent in the prepublished excerpt: the disruption of a sequence. "Faire paraître en revue la fin de *Sodome III*
avant qu'ait paru en volume *Sodome II*," he muses, "c'est bien
embrouiller le lecteur. Alors le mieux est peut-être de lui donner
[à Jacques Rivière] un fragment intégral de *Sodome II*" (It would
confuse the reader utterly if the end of *Sodome III* were published
in a journal before *Sodome II* appears in volume form. So the best
thing might be to offer [Jacques Rivière] an integral fragment of
Sodome II) (*Corr.*, 20:500). The "integral fragment," which Proust
proposes as an orderly measure against the disorder of fragmentation, is "integral" both because it is uncut and because it can be
reintegrated immediately into the text of the volume.

   As quite literal cuts in the fabric of the whole, excerpts posed
the *material* problem of putting the whole back together again. In
the same letter to Gallimard cited above, Proust complained of
being disrupted by the excerpts he had offered to Jacques Rivière
(for *La Nouvelle Revue Française*): "Il faut que j'aboutisse, et ses
fragments toujours coupés ça et là m'embrouillent extrêmement"
(I've got to get to the end of it, and his fragments always cut out
here and there confound me) (*Corr.*, 20:500). The excerpts for *Les
Œuvres libres*, on the other hand, were less disruptive because
taken as a single continuous ("integral") fragment: "Pour l'extrait
des *Œuvres libres* il y aurait peu à changer, car j'ai fait une large
coupure, mais je l'ai mise sous enveloppe et je n'aurai qu'à la
remplacer. En revanche, pour l'extrait de *La Nouvelle Revue
Française*, Jacques ayant coupé ça et là, ce sera toute une recon-

struction" (For the *Œuvres libres* excerpt there will be little to change, since I've cut out a sizable piece but have put it in an envelope and will only have to put it back in its place. On the other hand, for the *Nouvelle Revue Française* excerpt, since Jacques has cut a bit here and there, a whole reconstruction will be needed) (*Corr.*, 20:491–92).

Cutting, pasting, reconstructing: although this was precisely Proust's method of composition, he portrayed these editorial processes—cutting and pasting for nonliterary ends—as excessively taxing, even dangerous. "Pour une raison de même ordre, je ne puis lui donner [à Jacques Rivière] des extraits pour novembre, car ces extraits demandent des coupures, et après cela je ne sais plus comment rebouter le tout. Déjà les coupures du numéro d'octobre me donneront un genre de peine qui me fatigue bien plus que de composer" (For a similar kind of reason I cannot give him [Jacques Rivière] excerpts for November, since they would require cuts, after which I have no idea how to put the whole back together again. The cuts from the October issue will already demand a kind of labor that tires me much more than writing does) (*Corr.*, 20:479).[15] Excerpts belonged to the category of the editorial, along with other measures Proust construed as potentially harmful to the text as a whole—but necessary if his work was to go forth into the public realm. "Composer pour moi ce n'est rien," he insisted. "Mais rafistoler, rebouter, cela passe mon courage" (Writing is nothing for me, but patching back up, setting back together, I don't have the strength for it). The excerpts of *Sodome et Gomorrhe II* for *La Nouvelle Revue Française* must be free of cuts, he added, "sinon il faudra recommencer à rebouter, ce qui est mortel" (otherwise I'll have to start resetting things, which is deadly) (*Corr.*, 20:500–501). Proust used a similar register to evoke the dangers of a disruption in sequence. If *Le Côté de Guermantes II* was not ready for publication before *Sodome et Gomorrhe I*, "il serait funeste," he deplored, "que tout se chevauchât" (it would be disastrous [deadly] if everything overlapped) (*Corr.*, 20:54). *Mortel, funeste, mutiler:* Proust's allusions to the deadliness of fragmentation appear whenever the order or continuity of the living whole is threatened. It is in view of such a threat that he oversaw the text's material arrangement minutely, from beginning to end.

Indivisible

Over the years, *À la recherche du temps perdu* appeared in parts: as a series of volumes and in the form of excerpts, prepublications preceding each volume. Although Proust ultimately subjected his imagined continuous whole to fragmentation at every stage of its publication, he continued to prescribe, through his restrictions and specifications, a hermeneutical reading process for the entire work. As the text was divided into volumes, Proust's explicative discourse advised publisher and public alike that the "reality" of the *Recherche* was in its indivisibility, that its publication in separate parts failed to reflect its true unity.[16] Like the long letters that accompanied his manuscript when Proust first set out to find a publisher, these assertions of wholeness betray an anxiety over being misread. Just as the letters assert that the import of the book is to be found in the overall project, not in the particular manuscript, the discourse surrounding the publication of fragments or volumes affirms that the true *Recherche* is to be discovered not in its successive print appearances but rather in an underlying ideal work that has gradually yielded an original form as it has gone to press. How Proust might have imagined that ideal form can be deduced from the ways in which he resisted, from the beginning, the norms of early twentieth-century French publishing.

2 *The Dream of Simultaneous Publication*

> Mais est-ce un hasard si le livre est d'abord volume?
>
> But is it by accident that the book is, first and foremost, volume?
>
> —Jacques Derrida, "Force et signification"

When Proust proposed his manuscript to various publishers in the fall of 1912, it was without committing to a published form for the work other than the very one in which he delivered it: *Le Temps perdu* was an enormous stack of pages, an indivisible block. He had long since abandoned the idea of publication in serialized form, which would have circumvented the problem of division into volumes; now that his typescript had reached the unwieldy size of 712 pages, with more waiting to be transcribed, the question of how to divide up the work was inevitable.[1] It would finally impose itself as an unhappy confrontation with current editorial norms. Summing up this confrontation for a November 13, 1913, interview with Élie-Joseph Bois of *Le Temps*, Proust cast his novel as a tapestry too large for the walls of modern apartments—and himself as an anachronism. "J'aurais voulu publier le tout ensemble; mais on n'édite plus d'ouvrages en plusieurs volumes. Je suis comme quelqu'un qui a une tapisserie trop grande pour les appartements actuels et qui a été obligé de la couper" (I would have liked to publish the whole of it at once; but they don't publish works in several volumes anymore. I'm like someone who has a tapestry too large for modern apartments and has been forced to cut it). To cut a tapestry arbitrarily is of course to risk destroying the syntagmatic or symbolic relationships it represents. When Proust evoked the image of the tapestry again in his December 21 interview with *Le Miroir*'s André Arnyvelde (André Lévy), the emphasis moved from the excessive size of the tapestry to the inadequacy of the apartment as container: "Mon œuvre était dans ma pensée comme serait une vaste tapisserie dans un appartement qui ne pourrait la contenir" (In my mind, my work was like a vast tapestry in an apartment unable to contain it). Finally, looking back on the publication of *Du côté de chez Swann* in a letter to Gaston Gallimard some years later, Proust explained that since he was forced to cut his tapestry—"comme les gens qui ne disposent que d'un appartement trop petit" (like someone who has only a small apartment at his disposal)—for purely commercial reasons, it no longer mattered to him whether the text that remained was divided up into three or four volumes (Proust and Gallimard, *Correspondance*, 42).

It was Proust's initial resistance to the prospect of fragmentation that prompted him to seek publication by the Nouvelle Revue Française, the newly opened publishing wing of the literary journal (1911), whose director was Gaston Gallimard. The Nouvelle Revue Française, Proust imagined, less invested in the current practices of mainstream publishing, would respect his particular desires as to the form of the published work—that is to say, ultimately, the meaning of the project in its entirety. The story of his long search for a publisher is the unfolding of those particular desires, whose repeated assertion in the face of obstacles points to the persistence of an ideal: that of the single, indivisible whole.

When Proust first solicited the attention of Gallimard in November 1912, he had already met with rejection from two publishers, Alfred Vallette of *Le Mercure de France*—to whom he sent only a detailed letter explaining his project—and Gaston Calmette of *Le Figaro*, who ultimately failed to publish the novel in serialized form after promising to do so (see Chapter 1). It was his dealings with yet another publisher, Eugène Fasquelle, a major publisher who had survived the nineteenth-century downturn in book publishing, that finally forced him to confront the question of dividing his so-called indivisible work into volumes.[2] "Je suis très embarrassé pour la décision à prendre à l'égard de ce livre," Proust wrote to Georges de Lauris in March 1912. "Faut-il publier un volume de 800 à 900 pages[?] Un ouvrage en deux volumes de 400 pages chacun[?] Deux ouvrages de 400 pages chacun, ayant chacun un titre différent sous un même titre général[?] Ceci me plaît moins mais est plus agréable aux éditeurs" (I'm very perplexed about what decision I ought to take about the book. Should it be published as a single volume of 800 or 900 pages? As a work in two volumes of 400 pages each? Or two separate works of 400 pages, each with a different title, under the same general title? This I like less but it's what the publishers prefer) (*Corr.*, 11:76; *SL*, 3:63). The intermediate solution, a single work in several volumes, was counter to all editorial norms, as Proust would quickly discover. Fasquelle would no doubt impose different titles for each volume and an interval between their publication. "Cela m'ennuie beaucoup," Proust wrote to Louis de Robert, "mais on me dit qu'allieurs, ce serait la même chose. D'autre part je suis malade, très malade, par conséquent pressé de paraître, et Fasquelle a l'avantage . . . qu'il publiera (j'espère!) le livre immédiatement" (This bothers me a great deal, but I'm told that it would be the same elsewhere. On the other hand, I'm ill, very ill, and therefore in a hurry to appear, and Fasquelle has the advantage . . . of being prepared (I hope!) to publish the book immediately) (*Corr.*, 11:251; *SL*, 3:106).

Of these two constraints—on the one hand Proust's haste to publish, on the other his desire to control the conditions of publication—the latter wins out repeatedly: the fear that Fasquelle, a mainstream publisher, will impose his own normalizing practices leads Proust again and again to the same impasse. His first mention of the Nouvelle Revue Française, in an October 1912 letter to Louis de Robert, is tied specifically to the difficulty of publishing a single work in several volumes. Although in his interviews with the press he will later formulate his predicament in terms of his own obsolescence with respect to contemporary standards (see above), here Proust seems to place the problem of fragmentation under the sign of his novel's very modernity. "Croyez-vous que je ferais mieux de renoncer à l'idée de Fasquelle et qu'un éditeur purement littéraire (comme la Nouvelle Revue Française, qui consentirait peut-être à m'éditer en trois volumes . . .) aurait plus de chance de faire accepter des lecteurs un livre qui à vrai dire ne ressemble pas du tout au classique roman[?]" (Or do you think I would do better to give up the idea of Fasquelle and that a purely literary publisher [like the Nouvelle Revue Française who might perhaps agree to publish me in three volumes . . .] would be more likely to persuade readers to accept a work which it must be said is completely different from the classical novel?) (*Corr.*, 11:252; *SL*, 3:107). Returning to the question some months later in another letter to Robert, he adds: "Mais on me dit que cela ne se peut pas, qu'on n'achète plus, qu'on ne lit plus, un livre en plusieurs volumes" (But I've heard that it can't be done, that the public no longer buys, no longer reads, a book in several volumes) (*Corr.*, 12:224). Proust's oscillation between two contradictory perceptions—that he is out of date and that his time has not yet come—illuminates his paradoxical position during the initial search for a publisher. He correctly anticipates the difficulty of publishing a multivolume novel at the start of the twentieth century, but anxiously apprehends rejection of the work itself on the basis of its innovation. Fasquelle's rejection of Proust's manuscript, a decision made on the basis of a reader's report alone, will later confirm both of these apprehensions. "J'ai reçu une lettre de [Fasquelle] me disant qu'il ne croyait pas pouvoir assumer la publication d'un volume aussi considérable, aussi différent de ce que le public a l'habitude de lire" (I've received a letter from [Fasquelle] saying that he felt he could not undertake to publish a work of such length, and so different from what the public was accustomed to reading) (*Corr.*, 11:334; *SL*, 3:137).

When Proust refers to the details of publication as "the small side of things" in one of his letters to Robert, his words belie the veritable obsession with editorial detail that will soon become the hallmark of his dealings with publishers (*Corr.*, 12:224). A privileged object of Proust's concern is the interval between volumes—or rather its suppression. When at last he has resigned himself to the prospect of dividing the work into two or even three volumes, he proposes a series of measures that would re-create the material

unity of the single volume. In place of the continuity of the manuscript, he wishes to nullify the distance between volumes by
linking them in one of several ways: by a single title, by their
simultaneous publication, or, in the case of smaller volumes, by
having them sold together. Proposing to Georges de Lauris a single
work in two volumes of 400 pages each (see above), Proust specifies that the two volumes, appearing simultaneously, would be
unified by a general title. That the two volumes are a single work
becomes clear when he adds that there is no division to be made in
this case: "Je diviserai par deux le nombre total des pages et en
mettrai la moitié dans un volume, l'autre moitié dans l'autre" (I'd
simply divide the total number of pages by two and put half in one
volume and half in the other") (*Corr.*, 11:77; *SL*, 3:63). The volume
appears here as a simple measure, a capacity for so many pages, a
material unit that lends itself to a mathematical operation and
whose bounds do not coincide with those of an autonomous, harmonious narrative. The second solution he evokes—two volumes
with different titles—raises for Proust the specter of the interval.
"Seulement alors faudra-t-il," he queries Lauris, "laisser de l'in-
tervalle entre l'apparition des deux volumes[?] C'est bien contraire
à l'esprit du livre" (Only in that case should there be an interval
between the publication of the two volumes? It would be very
much against the spirit of the book) (*Corr.*, 11:76; *SL*, 3:63). Simultaneous publication emerges as the temporal substitute for the
imagined spatial continuity of the single volume.[3]

The same principle seems to be at work when Proust first
writes to Gaston Gallimard in November 1912, seeking an alternative to the publishing practices of Fasquelle—that is, to the likelihood that Fasquelle will impose different titles and an interval
between the publication of different volumes. Proust specifies to
Gallimard not only the number of pages each volume should have,
but the number of lines to a page, the number of characters to a line:
"Pouvez-vous faire des volumes ayant environ la longueur de 550
pages de trente-cinq lignes de quarante-cinq lettres[?]" (Can you
produce volumes of about 550 pages with thirty-five lines of forty-
five characters?) For the first volume, he adds, "il faudrait qu'il
paraisse *en une fois,* sinon [en] un seul tome, au moins en plusieurs
fascicules paraissant simultanément" (it would have to appear *all*

at once, if not in a single book, at least in several fascicles appearing simultaneously) (*Corr.*, 11:279; *SL*, 3:117, italics mine). *All at once* is seen to refer first to the material space of the volume, then to simultaneous publication of smaller fragments of text ("fascicles").

Proust's eventual acceptance of the inevitability of intervals brings with it a new proposal. Longer volumes can appear at fixed intervals, but smaller volumes must be joined together in such a way as to compensate for their separation. A 500-page volume, he writes to Louis de Robert, could be followed three to six months afterward by a second volume of 400 or 500 pages, with a third and final volume coming a year later; or perhaps together, he pursues, "par exemple dans un étui, deux de 350 pages pour commencer et, dans un an, deux autres ensemble de 350 pages" (for example in a case, two [volumes] of 350 pages to start with and, in a year, another two volumes of 350 sold together) (*Corr.*, 12:224). The greater the concession, the more insistently the tie between volumes returns in one form or another: the case or holder that would bind the volumes together externally is once again the suppression of the interval between (the reading of) them. Proust will later return to this idea of small volumes sold together in a case, after Bernard Grasset has become his publisher. *Du côté de chez Swann*, he writes to Madame de Pierrebourg in July 1913, could be published either as two volumes, with a first volume of 500 pages, or even as "trois petits volumes de 200 qu'on vendrait à la fois, dans une sorte d'étui" (three small volumes of 200 that would be sold at the same time, in a sort of case) (*Corr.*, 12:226). If fragmentation of some kind is inevitable, the work of reassembly will nonetheless resurface in the reading—provided only that the volumes sell. "Si je dois ne pas être lu, évidemment j'aime encore mieux que cela paraisse en loques et se recouse ensuite dans l'esprit du lecteur" (If I'm liable not to be read, obviously I'd prefer the thing to appear in tatters and be sewn up again in the reader's mind) (*Corr.*, 12:222; *SL*, 3:189).

Saying Everything at Once

Many critics have drawn a connection between the aesthetic theory elaborated in *Le Temps retrouvé* and a certain current of gallicized German Romantic philosophy that circulated in France

around the turn of the century, disseminating the aesthetic principles of Schiller, Schelling, and Schlegel. The most frequently cited
representative of this late nineteenth-century school of French
idealist philosophy is Gabriel Séailles, whose 1883 *Essai sur le
génie dans l'art* was the basis for an aesthetics course Proust
attended at the Sorbonne in 1894–95. Séailles's "philosophy of
genius"—which posits an initial moment of the creative process
as spontaneous, independent of personal will, and triggered by
sensation—has been suggested as a source and a model for Proust's
theory of involuntary memory.[4] But the legacy of *Le Génie dans
l'art* is perhaps more pertinently at work in the specifications,
interdictions, and eventual concessions that form the pattern
of Proust's resistance to the norms of the publishing world.
His defense of the *Recherche* as an indivisible whole can be read
as a narrative illustration of one of Séailles's key aesthetic principles: the putative simultaneity of conception, which lends to the
work of art a preliminary unity that will govern the development
of the parts.

Proust's repeated insistence on a symbolic separation between
two moments of the creative process (simultaneous composition
of beginning and end, followed by elaboration of the in-between)
corresponds to a precise theoretical problem formulated by
Séailles: the necessary dissociation of conception and execution.
"L'œuvre devrait jaillir d'un jet; ce n'est que l'impossibilité de tout
dire à la fois, ou la difficulté de l'expression, qui forcent l'artiste à
un travail successif. Dissimuler cette division, cette succession de
l'effort, donner l'illusion d'une exécution soudaine et simultanée,
dans chaque détail faire, si j'ose dire, l'œuvre tout entière, c'est là
tout le secret de l'art" (The work of art should spring forth in a
single jet; it is the impossibility of saying everything at once, or
the difficulty of expression, that force the artist to work succes-
sively. To disguise this division, this succession of efforts, to
reproduce in each detail the work as a whole, that is the entire
secret of art) (*Le Génie dans l'art*, 208). The impossibility of simultaneity—of "saying everything at once"—is at the heart of
Séailles's aesthetic theory, which conceives of the temporality of
process as an obstacle to be overcome. His formulation calls not
only for the dissimulation of successive effort, but for the creation

of an illusion of simultaneity that would disguise the inevitable separation between conception and execution.

Farther on, however, Séailles suggests that the problem of successivity resolves itself as though naturally from within the work itself, through a kind of automatic *compensation:* "L'exécution [de l'œuvre d'art] se fait simultanée, suppléé à l'impossibilité de jaillir d'un seul coup en se développant en tous sens" (The execution of the work of art makes itself simultaneous; it compensates for the impossibility of springing forth all at once by growing out in every direction) (212). Simultaneity is thus redefined as growth of the parts in relationship to one another, that is, as the internal logic behind the artist's necessarily successive efforts. It is successivity, then, not simultaneity, that is only an appearance. "Ces efforts, à vrai dire, sont simultanés, parce qu'ils sont tous en rapport, parce qu'ils se supposent les uns les autres" (These efforts, in reality, are simultaneous, since they exist in relationship to one another, since they all suppose one another) (213). Proust's frequent distinction between the "real book" and its outward appearance—the discrete, successive forms necessitated by the publication process—closely echoes Séailles's understanding of simultaneity.

It is the impossibility of saying everything at once, to take up Séailles's terms, that defers comprehension of *Du côté de chez Swann* to the end of the last volume. "[Mon sujet] est si vaste," Proust advises René Blum in November 1913, "qu'à peine l'aperçoit-on encore le premier volume fini" ([My subject] is so vast that one hardly gets a glimpse of it by the end of the first volume) (*Corr.,* 12:329). The visual metaphor that dominates Proust's descriptions of deferred comprehension dramatizes the paradox of textual successivity. The intervals inscribed in a successive reading—a reading over several volumes—represent arbitrary divisions in a whole that, according to the logic of the metaphor, should be taken in by the eye all at once. "Mon volume est un tableau. Il est vrai qu'un tableau est forcément *vu,* si grand qu'il soit, tandis qu'un livre ne se lit pas de la même manière" (My volume is a picture. It's true that a picture is necessarily *seen,* however large it is, whereas a book isn't read in the same way) (*Corr.,* 12:222; *SL,* 3:189). Proust's insistent ekphrasis will provide a consistent metaphor for his resistance to the division into volumes: he will lament one editorial decision after another as the slicing of a painting, the tearing of a tapestry.[5]

If Proust's brief correspondence with Gallimard at the end of 1912 sprang from his desire to find a more "literary" publisher than Fasquelle, his letters to both Fasquelle and Gallimard bear witness to the same apprehension of a rupture in the publication process. One or the other, he fears, will break off his engagement after the first volume, considering it a separate work. Proust evokes the possibility of such a rupture in his first letter to Fasquelle: "Si après le premier volume, vous cassiez mon œuvre en deux comme un vase qu'on brise, en en terminant là la publication . . ." (If after the first volume . . . you broke it in two like a shattered vase by ending its publication there . . .) (*Corr.*, 11:257; *SL*, 3:109–10). In his letters to Gallimard, Proust makes this point just as emphatically: "Bien entendu, je ne puis faire publier le premier volume, sans être sûr que le deuxième (ou deuxième et troisième, s'il y en a trois) seront publiés. Vous voyez d'ici ce que serait mon œuvre interrompue en pleine publication" (of course I can't let the first volume appear without being sure that the second [or the second and third if there are three] will be published. You can imagine what it would be like if my work were interrupted in the middle of publication) (*Corr.*, 11:285; *SL*, 3:119). Again Proust insists on the identity of the several volumes, imagining his work interrupted not as a text but as painting, tapestry, or vase. The division into volumes, the successivity of publication, is a form of violence—it is *couper, déchirer, briser* (cutting, ripping, breaking). To Gallimard, Proust describes the (projected) division into volumes as necessary but arbitrary; Gallimard's response must apply to the whole manuscript, he insists, "car vous comprenez comme il ne s'agit pas de deux ouvrages mais d'un seul coupé arbitrairement en deux à cause de la longueur, je ne peux pas rester en plan après le premier volume" (for as you realize it isn't two books but one, cut arbitrarily in two because of its length, and I cannot be left stranded after the first volume) (*Corr.*, 11:321; *SL*, 3:129).

The danger of an interrupted publication, which Proust evokes repeatedly in his correspondence with would-be publishers, similarly motivates his attempt at this time to establish regular intervals between volumes rather than suppressing them. If the first volume appears in February or March (1913), the second should appear only in November, he specifies to Gallimard, "pour laisser l'assimilation d'un aussi gros morceau se faire normalement" (to allow for normal assimilation of such a large section), and the third the following February (*Corr.*, 11:286). This contractual spacing of intervals will assure continued publication of the necessarily discrete volumes. Whether Proust's strategy is to suppress or to regulate the temporal spacing of volumes, the meaning of the gesture is the same. The separate volumes must be linked together, either by their simultaneous publication or by the inscription of the interval, like the excerpt, into the reading process. The proposed eight-month gap between the first and second volumes, allowing for absorption of the material and preparing the reader for further reading, is analogous in this sense to the "homeopathic" publication of excerpts in *Le Figaro* (see Chapter 1). But this strategic use of the editorial interval obscures the fact that the ideal reading prescribed by Proust is *precisely* a reading by intervals: the interval between a misleading first impression and its rectification, between an apparently useless detail and its justification. Proust's system of *preparations* is in effect the inscription of intervals—sometimes over several volumes—into reading.[6] What he confronts in the publication process is the possibility of the arbitrary interval, the division of the work along a linear axis. His resistance to cutting the text can be seen as an effort to preserve the intermittency demanded by reading itself.

Since the editorial interval is both division and delay—fragmentation into volumes and the hiatus between their publication—Proust will finally come to use this delay as a positive structure to lend rhythm and order to successive publication. The interval between volumes can be seen not only as a necessary part of the reading process, but as a way of providing time for the revision and completion of future volumes announced. Appropriated as part of a strategy, the interval eventually coincides with Proust's own patterns of delay. In his final projection, in 1921, of "quatre longs volumes qui se succéderont à intervalles assez espacés (si Dieu me prête vie)" (four long volumes to follow at fairly long intervals [if God grants me life]), the interval has become dramatically inseparable from the time needed to finish each volume (*Corr.*, 20:53; *SL*, 4:186).

Voluminous

In his 1912 correspondence with Fasquelle and then Gallimard, Proust attempted to negotiate the material details of publication as though one and then the other had already signed on as his publisher. In reality, of course, his letters were merely tentative efforts to get their attention. Both Fasquelle and the Nouvelle Revue Française sent their letters of rejection in December 1912; Proust received them within two days of one another.[7] The next rejection would come from the director of the Librairie Ollendorff, Alfred Humblot, who complained in a much-quoted letter that he could not understand how a man could take thirty pages to describe how he shifts about in bed before falling asleep (the letter was addressed to Louis de Robert, Proust's intermediary, but Robert passed it on to him). Proust deplored Humblot's miscomprehension, explaining to Robert that the first chapter proceeded by withholding and deferral: "J'ai en effet essayé d'envelopper mon premier chapitre . . . dans des impressions de demi-réveil dont la signification ne sera complète que plus tard" (I've tried, as a matter of fact, to bathe my first chapter in impressions of semi-wakefulness whose meaning will become clear only later on) (*Corr.*, 12:84). It was in February 1913 that Proust finally turned to René Blum to ask him to serve as an intermediary in soliciting the attention of Bernard Grasset—with five rejections behind him.

In his first letter to Blum, Proust at once evokes the gravity of his illness (and hence his haste to publish) and stipulates that if Grasset agrees to publish the work, it must be published at the author's expense.[8] In an extended metaphor that identifies the work with the dying self and publication with interment, Proust separates the *œuvre* from its anticipated published form and assigns to the work a will. "Je travaille depuis longtemps à cette œuvre, j'y ai mis le meilleur de ma pensée; elle réclame maintenant un tombeau qui soit achevé avant que le mien soit rempli et en m'aidant à accomplir son vœu vous faites pour moi quelque chose de précieux" (I've been working on this book for a long time and have put the best of myself into it; now it is clamoring for a tomb that can be completed before mine is filled, and in helping me to fulfill its wish you will be doing something that is for me beyond price) (*Corr.*, 12:80; *SL*, 3:150). The identification of the published form with the tomb suggests, of course, the Renaissance tradition of the *tombeau*—a poetic work composed in honor of a dead author—as well as signifying a text completed and laid to rest. Proust's insistence on publishing at his own expense gives additional meaning to the wish (*vœu*) for a finished form that he attributes to his work—and which he hopes Blum will help to fulfill: "Si Monsieur Grasset édite le livre à ses frais, il va le lire, me faire attendre, me proposera des changements, de faire des petits volumes, etc. Et aura raison au point de vue du succès. Mais je recherche plutôt la claire présentation de mon œuvre" (If Monsieur Grasset publishes the book at his expense, he will read it, make me wait, suggest changes, smaller volumes, etc. And he'll be right from the point of view of sales. But what I am looking for is rather the clear presentation of my work) (*Corr.*, 12:80; *SL*, 3:151). What Proust metaphorizes as the work's own will is not merely a will to publication but also the assertion of authorial will in opposition to the anticipated imposition of editorial will. Perhaps the most remarkable aspect of Proust's anticipation of editorial intervention is the first concern he expresses: the publisher will *read the manuscript*. Whereas his earlier communications with publishers, like the long letter to Fasquelle that accompanied the manuscript, were intended precisely to make (editorial) reading— and subsequently publication—possible, here publication depends instead upon the publisher's effacement as reader. The prospective publisher has become, according to the expression of Lhomeau and Coelho, a "technician of the book" (*Marcel Proust*, 119).

In fact, it is only after Proust has concluded a deal with Grasset that he sends him a manuscript, along with a few excerpts published by *Le Figaro*. In an accompanying letter he suggests to Grasset that if he doesn't wish to read the manuscript, the excerpts will at least give him an idea (rather inexact, he adds) of its form (*Corr.*, 12:97). Despite Proust's earlier caution regarding excerpts, which he feared would supplant the reading process, here he proposes excerpts to Grasset precisely to replace reading. In this light, his assertion to René Blum that he is seeking the "clear presentation" of his work must be understood as pertaining to the public alone. The will to control the reading process, which emerged early on in his detailed letters to publishers, has now become a question of *presentation:* the publisher's role is to make the work accessible in giving it a viable format, for which task comprehension of the project—and reading of the manuscript— are no longer prerequisites.

Proust's contractual negotiations with Grasset in the spring of 1913 bring about new strategies for reconstituting the indivisible whole that he imagined as the ideal material form for *Le Temps perdu.* He proposes to Grasset a work in two parts and sets a limit to the length of the first volume: the recurring figure is 700 pages. Both his refusal to divide the manuscript into smaller, more accessible volumes and his reluctance to pass the 700-page threshold are striking. Proust will relinquish the idea of the seven hundred-page volume only under editorial pressure, and only after he has tried in a variety of ways to contort the lengthy manuscript into the size and shape of the projected volume. He justifies his insistence on a lengthy first volume in terms of his system of *preparations,* explaining to Grasset that "les préparations sont si lentes dans ce premier volume qu'il y a avantage à conduire le lecteur aussi loin que possible afin qu'il commence un peu à se débrouiller" (the preparations are so slow in this first volume that it's advisable to take the reader as far as possible so that he can begin to find his way a bit) (*Corr.,* 12:99; *SL,* 3:162, translation modified). This desire to preserve the lengthiness of the first volume is one of two irreconcilable conditions that drive the negotiation of a contract with Grasset: that the volume be readable (in Proust's terms) and that it be accessible—unlike Calmann-Lévy's luxury edition of *Les Plaisirs et les jours.* The volume's accessibility will depend on two factors, price and format; Proust suggests a price of three and a half francs. It is the second factor, however, that is at the heart of the problem of accessibility. A volume of seven hundred pages is, as Bernard Grasset puts it, "de circulation difficile" (*Corr.,* 13:394).

The attempt to reconcile these contradictory desires takes the form of textual compression. In each of his efforts to force the lengthy text into the space of a normative volume size, Proust aims to redistribute its mass without further cutting. In order that this first volume not be too "voluminous," he writes, it should contain "beaucoup de lignes et les lignes beaucoup de lettres" (many lines, and the lines many characters) (*Corr.*, 12:96). In his 1912 correspondence with Gallimard, Proust suggested that each of his two volumes should approximate Flaubert's *Éducation sentimentale*. He now proposes Zola's *Travail* as a model, enclosing an actual copy of the book with his letter to Grasset—as though to legitimate his expectation of publishing a volume of similarly formidable dimensions. The format offered by *Travail* could be expanded, he suggests, from 45 letters per line to 50, 35 lines per page to 36, for a total of up to 700 pages. Each of Proust's two volumes would be "analogous" to the one he encloses (*Corr.*, 12:99), he adds, precisely as though the volume were a standard mold into which the manuscript—the "material," as he calls it—would be poured for publication. Zola's *Travail*, however, is not a standard volume. It is Louis de Robert who brings this to his friend's attention, in a letter advising him that Zola was able to publish a volume of such daunting size only by virtue of his reputation.[9] Proust is not unaware that his own situation prior to the publication of *Swann* is entirely different. In a letter of the same period, he recognizes that he has lived so far outside of literary circles that he is, even at his age, "plus inconnu que tant de débutants" (more unknown than so many first-time authors) (*Corr.*, 12:351). What is striking about the models Proust has chosen is their inappropriateness: he has neither the reputation of a Zola nor the nineteenth-century public of Flaubert.

Before the length of *Du côté de chez Swann* is definitively set, Proust will continue to propose new ways of altering the distribution of the material so as to compress it into the space of the imagined volume. After making extensive corrections on the first set of proofs, he insists on having the text printed in a nearly continuous block, with no indentations for dialogues. To Grasset he describes this suppression of blank spaces as a possible "contraction" of the text. To Louis de Robert, he writes: "Pour gagner de la place, j'ai fait supprimer les blancs dans tous les dialogues. Grasset trouve cela laid. Moi je trouve cela mieux, cela fait entrer davantage les propos dans la continuité du texte" (To save space, I've omitted blank spaces in all of the dialogues. Grasset thinks it's ugly. I think it's better. It assimilates the dialogues into the continuity of

the text) (*Corr.*, 12:212). (Proust's indentations for new paragraphs
were so rare that Theodor Adorno would later comment on his
"stubborn and abyssal passion for writing without paragraphs. He
was irritated by the demand for comfortable reading, which forces
the graphic image to serve up small crumbs that the greedy cus-
tomer can swallow more easily, at the cost of the continuity of the
material itself" ["Bibliographical Musings," 30].) Proust even asks
Robert to mark what he calls the text's *longueurs*—so that they
can be omitted or put into footnotes (*Corr.*, 12:211). But the idea of
footnotes, along with that of the 700-page volume, is thoughtfully
discouraged by Louis de Robert. Citing the short attention span of
the early twentieth-century reader, he advises Proust that a volume of 700 pages will be simply skimmed over by the reader's eyes
(*Corr.*, 12:219).

Longer than Zola: Ending Du côté de chez Swann

Georges de Lauris, in his preface to the collection of letters from
Proust he published in 1948, wrote of the reception of *Du côté de
chez Swann:*

> Des critiques ont reproché à Marcel de ne point choisir, de tout
> dire. Il prétendait, au contraire, que le propre de l'artiste est juste-
> ment de choisir entre tous les traits que sa mémoire et son imag-
> ination lui proposent. Le plan de son œuvre, avec les parties qui se
> répondent les unes aux autres, les thèmes qui reviennent en se
> renouvelant, lui apparaissait, je crois, comme celui d'une sym-
> phonie (*A un ami*, 32–33).

> Critics reproached Marcel for not choosing, for saying everything.
> He claimed, on the contrary, that the defining activity of an artist
> was precisely to choose among all the features that his memory
> and his imagination proposed to him. The structure of his work,
> with all of its parts corresponding to one another, appeared to
> him, I believe, like that of a symphony.

The reproach to which Lauris refers can be found in a scathing
reader's report submitted to Fasquelle by Jacques Normand, a the-
ater critic who published under the pseudonym "Madeleine" (it
was on the basis of this report that Fasquelle rejected the manu-

script). The exasperation of Normand before the lengthy text is palpable in every line. At the end of 712 pages, he writes, "on n'a
aucune notion de quoi il s'agit" (one has no idea at all what it's
about). He describes the volume as "excessive" and as "plus long
qu'un des plus longs romans de Zola" (longer than one of Zola's
longest novels), drawing precisely the comparison Proust will suggest when he chooses Zola's *Travail* as a model volume. Normand's
criticism of the volume's excessiveness is formulated specifically
in terms of the arbitrariness of Proust's proposal to end the volume
at page 633: "L'auteur concède que son premier volume pourrait
s'arrêter à la page 633. Il n'y a pas d'inconvénient; et il n'y a pas d'a-
vantage, car à quatre vingts pages près, sur le nombre!" (The author
concedes that his first volume could end at page 633. There's no
reason why not; and there's no reason why, for what's a difference
of eighty pages, out of a zillion!). From the arbitrariness of the volume ending, Normand draws out a larger implication: "Et d'autre
part, il n'y a pas de raison pour que l'auteur n'ait pas doublé ou
même décuplé son manuscrit. Étant donné le procédé de 'dégoiser
pendant des heures, chemin faisant' qu'il emploie, écrire vingt volumes est aussi normal que de s'arrêter à un ou à deux" (And
besides, there is no reason why the author should not have doubled
his manuscript or even multiplied it tenfold. Given his practice of
"rattling on for hours en route," writing twenty volumes would be
just as normal as stopping at one or two).[10]

This reproach touches upon a problem that will present a continual obstacle as Proust attempts to bring a finished work into the
public realm: the movement that impels the text forward, generat-
ing ever more material, provides no inherent pattern for endings.
Proust's repeated proposal of Flaubert's and Zola's texts as models
to which his own volume should conform can be seen in the light
of this search for an arrested form that must be imposed from without. It is only through editing that the work will be "arrested"
(arbitrarily, says Proust), its content "exhausted" by the volume.
Proust's opposition between the *œuvre* and its published form, evident throughout his correspondence with Grasset, emerges here as
a distinction between what he calls the "real content" of the volume and the volume itself—which he construes as a material
limit. In a letter written to Henry Bordeaux a few months before

the publication of *Swann*, Proust sums up his understanding of his dilemma. "J'espère qu'un jour finira par paraître le gros livre que j'ai écrit, et par lequel vous me connaîtrez mieux, mais il ne pourra paraître en un volume faute de volumes assez gros" (I hope one day the big book I've written, through which you'll come to know me better, will see the light of day, but it can't be published in one volume due to lack of volumes large enough) (*Corr.*, 12:142). The fault—to take up Proust's locution literally—lies not with the length of the text, but with the purely external *volume*, which fails to contain the text. His proposal of Zola's *Travail* can be understood in similar terms: emptied of its text, it might be voluminous enough to contain the *Recherche*. The volume is, in short, an imaginary structure independent of the text. Ending the volume means orchestrating a coincidence between the external form of the volume and the internal logic of the work itself. This can be done only by finding, as Proust puts it, a "pedal point" (*point d'orgue*) where the novel can be temporarily suspended.

The term appears in a letter to Grasset in which Proust objects that his wish to suppress blank spaces within the text is not at all a question of aesthetic preference. It is, rather, a *material necessity* that will affect the economy of the entire work. If dialogues are not integrated into the text, he warns Grasset, they will arrive at a volume of considerable length "sans que la matière du premier tome soit achevée" (without exhausting the material of the first volume). What Proust envisions in this case is nothing short of a complete rearrangement of the entire novel: every part of the whole will be affected by a change in the length of *Swann*. In a perfect illustration of Séailles's "law of organic correlation," Proust explains that if the 700-page limit is to be passed, "il y a avantage à le savoir parce que cela modifiera forcément les titres des parties etc., l'économie totale se trouvant modifiée pour que l'équilibre ne soit pas rompu" (we're better off knowing it, since it will necessarily modify the titles of the different parts, etc., the total economy adapting to the change so as not to break the balance of the whole).[11] The "pedal point" or "organ point," in musical terms a point of stasis and tension produced by the prolongation of a note at will, then appears as a way of preventing the rupture Proust fears in the harmony of the whole. "Je trouverai toujours bien un 'point d'orgue' où arrêter ce premier volume si tout son contenu réel n'est pas épuisé quand son extrême limite de dimension matérielle sera atteinte" (I can always find a "pedal point" at which to stop the volume if all its real content is not exhausted when its outermost material limit is reached) (*Corr.*, 12:190).

In the pedal point metaphor is an assertion of meaning that opposes the carefully orchestrated pause or "ending" to the simple division or "end." In July 1913, when Proust sees that the threshold of 700 pages has indeed been passed, he writes to Grasset that he must find a suitable ending to form a shorter volume but that "une fin n'est pas une simple terminaison et . . . je ne peux pas couper cela aussi facilement qu'une motte de beurre" (an ending is not a simple termination and . . . I cannot cut the book as easily as a lump of butter) (*Corr.*, 12:233; *SL*, 3:185). The complete meaninglessness of the simple "end" (*terminaison*), evoked by the image of the lump of butter, is underscored by the elaborate system of meaning that Proust constructs around the "ending" (*fin*). It is nothing short of "impossible," for example, to end the volume just after the first part ("Combray"), unless the second part is sold together with it—thus nullifying the division (*Corr.*, 12:218). To Louis de Robert, Proust insists: "Quand vous aurez lu les épreuves de l'ancien premier volume, vous vous rendrez compte qu'en tous cas il est impossible de le terminer avant la page 550 ou 520" (When you've read the proofs of the original first volume, you'll realize that in any case it is impossible to end it before page 550 or 520) (*Corr.*, 12:224). But Proust's objections come up against Grasset's acute sense for literary marketing: Grasset vetoes each of Proust's proposed strategies in favor of publishing a presentable, autonomous volume. "Il faut qu'un livre soit 'un livre,'" he admonishes Proust, "c'est-à-dire une chose complète, se suffisant à elle-même. Le problème de la fragmentation ne peut donc être résolu que par vous-même" (A book must be "a book," that is, a thing complete unto itself. The problem of fragmentation can thus be resolved by you alone) (*Corr.*, 13:394). As a result of Grasset's insistence that a book must be a book, Proust will have to lend *Swann* what he calls a "premature ending." Curtailing the typescript he has given to Grasset, he then adds on five or six pages from the second volume in order to create, as he writes to Robert, "un couronnement un peu plus étendu" (a slightly more extended climax) (*Corr.*, 12:271; *SL*, 3:206).[12]

The final version of *Du côté de chez Swann* comprises the three familiar chapters "Combray," "Un Amour de Swann," and "Noms de pays: Le Nom"; Proust has omitted a last chapter, "Noms de pays." The meaning of this premature ending is suggested in an earlier letter to Robert in which Proust proposes various titles for the volume (in response to Robert's vigorous objection to "Du côté de chez Swann"): "Jardins dans une tasse de thé," "L'Âge des noms," or "Charles Swann." His preference, he adds, would go to "Charles Swann"—but if the volume must be cut back to 500 pages, he would indicate that it's not all of Swann: "*Premiers crayons de Charles Swann*" (First strokes in the drawing of Charles Swann) (*Corr.*, 12:232). The prematurely ended volume sketches out the story of Swann, so to speak, without completing it. The image recalls the oft-repeated prescription for genius attributed to Séailles's *maître* Félix Ravaisson: that a painting must be painted with a single brush-stroke.[13] In Séailles's formulation the single stroke, proceeding from unity of inspiration, is reconstituted by illusion. For Proust the shortened *Swann* is the stroke suspended in midair, broken by the successivity of publication. After the length of the volume is finally fixed at 523 pages, Proust repeatedly declares in his letters that it ends arbitrarily, "sans queue ni tête" (with neither head nor tail). The 523-page volume represents, he seems to suggest, a victory of the editorial over the literary.[14]

Du côté de chez Swann appeared on the shelves November 14, 1913—some seven months after Proust's originally projected date of publication. In his very first letter to Grasset, Proust had articulated his desire that the first volume appear in May and his fear that this might be "materially impossible" (*Corr.*, 12:96). By the time *Swann* was actually in press, the meaning of this impossibility had become clear: Proust's last-minute revision of the ostensibly finished text was nothing short of a complete rewriting. The extent of his corrections to the galley-proofs can be surmised from his frequent references to a supplement of 595 francs charged by his publisher to cover the expense of printing the corrected text. It was no understatement when Proust wrote to Louis de Robert, after submitting the first set of proofs, "j'ai récrit sur épreuves un nouveau livre" (I've written a new book on the proofs themselves) (*Corr.*, 12:212).

Although Proust begins with an announcement of haste to publish—"je suis malade, très malade, par conséquent pressé de paraître" (I am ill, very ill, and therefore in a hurry to appear) (*Corr.*, 11:251; *SL*, 3:106)—the moment of publication, of the arrested form, is continually pushed away by a refusal to separate from the text. The correction of proofs, an activity that occupied a good part of Proust's final years, takes its place as a third term in what I have called the agonistic structure that presided over the beginning of the writing process (see Chapter 1). His announcements of beginnings are inseparable from the specter of a premature death, but it is the monumental task of self-editing that prevents him from arriving at a final form. The "new book" that emerges from Proust's corrections on the proofs of his first volume provides a paradigm for a writing process in which the word *fin* nearly always marks a new point of departure. This renewed and seemingly endless growth determines a pattern of announcement and delay that begins with the publication of *Swann* and will continue until his death.

In a letter to critic André Beaunier soon after the appearance of *Swann*, Proust warned him not to wait for the succeeding volumes to appear in 1914 as announced on the book's flyleaf—an announcement made only at his publisher's insistence, he added, and in order to whet the reader's appetite. The reference to future volumes is followed, characteristically, by a reference to his failing health. "Mais en admettant même que ma santé me permette de mettre au point tout cet ensemble, ce n'est pas avant trois ou quatre ans qu'il pourra être sur pied. Tout est écrit," he continued, in a formula strikingly similar to his 1909 announcement to Madame Straus, "mais tout est à reprendre" (But even supposing that my health allows me to finish the whole thing, it won't be up and running for three or four years. Everything is written, but everything is to be rewritten) (*Corr.*, 12:367). Proust's second pronouncement that "everything is written" reflects the reality of the text in a way that the first does not, since the three-volume *Recherche* clearly constitutes a whole. But in the passage from one announcement of completion to the next—the first referring principally to the structure of the book to come, the second to three actual volumes of material—the scope of revision has grown with the text itself: "everything is to be rewritten." In effect, the closer the *Recherche* comes to completion, the more it is subject to new development and therefore to further delay; the more Proust has produced, the smaller the likelihood he will fulfill his program of publishing a completed work before death.

In this light, Proust's insistence on simultaneity takes on a new density. His repeated efforts to preserve the form of the single volume, or to ensure the simultaneous appearance of several volumes, can be read as a response to Séailles's recommendation that the entire secret of art is in the dissimulation of successivity. The drama of Proust's initial encounter with publishing in 1912–13 suggests that unity can be reinscribed in the text only through the successivity of reading—that is, through a system of delays. The delay in reading, from first impression to comprehension, from first volume to last, contains a promise of future meaning that would turn successivity back into simultaneity by leading the reader to a hermeneutical moment in which everything will be accounted for.[15]

Another test of Proust's claims awaited him, however. In the gap between conception and execution, between one announcement of forthcoming volumes and the next, lay real time with its endless possibilities for revision, its contingencies and its accidents. We turn now to Proust's encounter with the unforeseen revisions of life itself.

3   *Organicism Gone Awry*

La plupart des monstres le sont avec symétrie,
le dérangement des parties paraît s'être fait avec
ordre.

Most monsters are symmetrically monstrous:
the disordering of their parts appears to have taken
place in an orderly way.

—Buffon, *Supplément à l'histoire naturelle*

When Jacques Normand, in his reader's report for
Eugène Fasquelle in 1912, wrote of Proust's meandering manuscript that "écrire vingt volumes est aussi normal que de s'arrêter
à un ou à deux" (writing twenty volumes would be just as normal
as stopping at one or two), *Le Temps perdu* comprised only two
volumes. By 1927, with the publication of the posthumous volumes by the Nouvelle Revue Française, the number would expand
to sixteen. In his oddly prophetic remark, Normand not only
anticipates the novel's eventual expansion but also formulates, on
the basis of the one volume he has read, a particular criticism that
will follow the *Recherche* from the moment *Du côté de chez
Swann* appears in 1913: it will be deemed excessive, disproportionate, even monstrous. Although Proust will never see the
reader's report in question, he seems to be responding to its very
terms when he writes to Louis de Robert, after receiving Fasquelle's
rejection, that he is thinking of proposing to Fasquelle a collection
of his articles from *Le Figaro* "en un petit volume qui n'aura rien,
lui, d'anormal et de démesuré" (in a small volume which would be

in no way abnormal or inordinate in length) (*Corr.*, 11:335; *SL*, 3:138). In the midst of Proust's continual assertions to friends and prospective publishers that his book is not a collection but an *ouvrage*, a whole work, it is the collection or *petit volume* that emerges as a measured alternative to the text's *démesure*. What's more, Proust's implication that the difficulty of publishing his lengthy work is a question of norms and measures—that it will be seen as both abnormal and *démesuré* (excessive, disproportionate)—not only echoes the terms of the reader's report submitted to Fasquelle, but anticipates an important element in the later reception of *À la recherche du temps perdu:* an ongoing reference to lack of measure, disproportion, departure from norms.

Proust is not alone in proposing a small volume or collection as an antidote to the perceived excessiveness of his lengthy manuscript. In a December 1913 review for *Le Temps* that has come to represent the initial reception of *Du côté de chez Swann*, critic Paul Souday writes: "Il nous semble que le gros volume de Monsieur Marcel Proust n'est pas composé, et qu'il est aussi démesuré que chaotique, mais qu'il renferme des éléments précieux dont l'auteur aurait pu former un petit livre exquis" (It seems to me that Monsieur Marcel Proust's thick volume has no structure, and that it's as excessive as it is chaotic; but it encloses precious elements from which the author could have made a small, exquisite book).[1] Souday's imagined collection brings to mind precisely the reputation for preciosity that Proust is trying to overcome with the publication of *Swann*, and whose charge is present for him in words such as *précieux* and *exquis* (as well as *délicat* and *fin*, as we saw above). In Lucien Maury's December 27 article for *La Revue politique et littéraire*, Souday's "small, exquisite book" becomes "quatre ou cinq petits livres qui, séparés, eussent paru distingués, charmants, sans peut-être revendiquer une gloire exceptionnelle" (four or five small books which, published separately, would have appeared distinguished, charming, perhaps without meriting exceptional recognition). For Maury, Proust's volume is an amalgam out of which one might extract "un recueil de sentences et de maximes morales, un florilège de dissertations sur l'art et la vie, une galerie de portraits et de tableaux de mœurs, une autre galerie de paysages lyriques, voire un petit roman languissant" (a collection of moral adages and maxims, a florilegium of theses on art and life, a gallery of portraits and paintings of manners, another gallery of lyrical landscapes, even a brief languid novel) (Lhomeau and Coehlo, *Marcel Proust,* 300). Proust's success in publishing a continuous volume, then—which he continually opposed to the collection of articles, the serial novel, or successive excerpts—has resulted in a return of the very terms he has sought to exclude. What he sees as integral to the continuous work is separated out by critics and reconfigured as an ideal imaginary work, the "brief languid novel," the "collection of maxims." The volume thus reimagined as a collection of elements would preclude, through its selection, the excessiveness by which the *gros volume*—to take up Paul Souday's expression—errs.

These immediate critical responses illustrate the kind of reading Proust hoped to discourage by his warnings, exhortations, and promises of hermeneutically discovered meaning: a short-sighted reading that fails to perceive the necessity of the parts, and especially a reading that construes *Swann* as an amalgam of dissociable fragments. "Je vois pour ma part," Lucien Maury continues, "que Marcel Proust a voulu tenter une addition dont il n'a pas su réaliser le total" (For my part, I see that Marcel Proust has tried to perform an addition but has missed the total sum): for Maury, "addition" is the (nonorganic) process according to which Proust tries, and fails, to construct his novel. A similar charge appears in Henri Ghéon's review for the January 1, 1914, issue of *La Nouvelle Revue Française.* Echoing Souday, Ghéon suggests that Proust has failed to observe the doctrine of organic form. "Monsieur Marcel Proust, au lieu de se résumer, de se contracter, s'abandonne. . . . Il ne prend même pas la peine d'être logique et encore moins de 'composer.' Cette satisfaction organique, que nous procure une œuvre dont nous embrassons d'un regard tous les membres, la forme, il nous la refuse obstinément" (Marcel Proust, instead of summarizing, condensing, lets himself go. . . . He doesn't even go to the trouble of being logical and even less so of "composing." That organic satisfaction offered by a work of art whose limbs and form we take in at a single glance, he obstinately refuses to give it to us) (Lhomeau and Coelho, *Marcel Proust,* 308). If Ghéon's description of the work of art whose "limbs" we can take in at a single glance recalls the

Aristotelian prescription that a beautiful object should be "readily taken in at one view" (*Poetics*, 14), it also seems to give justification to Proust's initial refusal to divide his 1,500-page manuscript for fear of jeopardizing reader comprehension.[2]

The terms in which Ghéon describes Proust's failure to construct an organically sound work are noteworthy in themselves. Above, he attributes the text's lack of organic structure to willfulness and obstinacy on the part of the author; elsewhere in the same review, he accuses Proust precisely of failing to assert will in the composition process: Proust "refuses" readers organic satisfaction, but "refuses" (himself) nothing in his choice of material. "N'ayant pas à juger, il n'a pas eu à refuser; il n'a refusé rien . . . Ainsi, la moindre image de rencontre, le moindre souffle printanier, comme le moindre passant de la rue, ont pris dans sa mémoire une place aussi grande et non moins privilégiée que les plus rares aventures, que les plus déchirantes passions, que les êtres les plus attachés à sa vie. Loin de lui le dessein de choisir et de 'préférer' dans tout cela! Toutes choses sont égales" (Since he doesn't have to make judgments, he hasn't had to exclude anything; he has excluded nothing [*n'a refusé rien*] . . . Thus the least little image of an encounter, like the slightest passer-by in the street, have taken on in his memory a place as large and as privileged as the rarest adventures, the most agonizing passions, and the most important people in his life. Far be it from him to choose and to "prefer" in all of this! Every single thing carries equal weight) (Lhomeau and Coelho, *Marcel Proust,* 307). *Du côté de chez Swann,* Ghéon concludes, is not a novel: "C'est une 'somme,' la somme d'observations, de sensations et de sentiments, la plus complexe que notre âge nous ait livrée" (It's a "sum," the sum of observations, of sensations and of feelings, the most complex sum that our era has ever given us). He then effectively turns *Swann* into a collection of discrete texts by assimilating it to Montaigne's *Essais*: it should be read, he suggests, *"page à page,* à temps perdu, comme on lit les *Essais"* (page by page, at one's leisure, just as one reads the *Essais*) (Lhomeau and Coelho, *Marcel Proust,* 310). Ghéon's response typifies the initial reception of *Swann* by presenting the text as assemblage, amalgam, or sum. The comparison with Montaigne even suggests an *inde-pendence of the page*—which is precisely the hallmark, in late nineteenth-century terms, of a "decadent" style.[3]

Read in conjunction with Ghéon's remarks, Souday's review clearly emerges as belonging to the same nineteenth-century register. The story of Charles Swann, he claims, is *excessive* ("un énorme épisode, occupant la bonne moitié du volume" [one enormous episode, occupying a good half of the volume]) and suffers from the same lack of internal structure as Ghéon's "sum" ("Et que d'épisodes dans cet épisode!" [And what a lot of episodes in this episode!]). To the independence of the page, the sentence, and the word, Souday adds that of the *episode*. Finally, Souday qualifies Proust as "un nerveux, un sensuel, et un rêveur" (an over-sensitive type, a sensualist, and a dreamer), terms that resonate directly with the critiques formulated by Paul Bourget against Huysmans and other "decadents" whose "impressionism" (as Bourget called it) was marked by a privileging of sensation.[4] Souday concludes his review with the hope of discovering in the next volume "un peu plus d'ordre, de brièveté, et un style plus châtié" (a little more order and concision, and a more chastened style) (Lhomeau and Coelho, *Marcel Proust,* 287).

The reviews in question here, which appeared within a few months of the publication of *Du côté de chez Swann,* from November 1913 to February 1914 (with the exception of Normand's unpublished reader's report), have two things in common. First, they constitute an unwittingly perverse response to Proust's long struggle with the prospect of fragmentation and his efforts to dissociate *Swann* from *Les Plaisirs et les jours:* they tend to break down the integral, continuous work into its constituent elements and to prefer the collection—the precious treasury of maxims, portraits, poetry, theories, or even, in the words of Ghéon, "documents on modern hypersensitivity" (Lhomeau and Coelho, *Marcel Proust,* 310)—to the continuity of the volume. They also tax Proust with a failure to choose between the "thousand and one details" that occur to him, as the novelist Rachilde put it in her review for *Le Mercure de France* (Lhomeau and Coelho, *Marcel Proust,* 311). What is peculiarly appropriate about these critical responses is that they replicate the problematic that dominated Proust's own experience with writing and seeking publication: the problem of where and how to stop and end. Accordingly, they offer different models for "stopping" a text perceived as chaotic and verbose, for imposing selection where it seems no choice has been asserted. Jacques Normand, for his part, proposes a model of simple mathematical reduction ("tout cela pourrait être réduit de moitié, des trois quarts, des neuf dixièmes" [all of that could be reduced by half, by three-fourths, by nine-tenths]) (Lhomeau and Coelho, *Marcel Proust*, 261). In short, the early reception of *Swann* seemed to confirm Bernard Grasset's terse assessment of Proust's first volume as "unreadable." "C'est illisible," he confided to a friend just after its publication, "nous l'avons publié à compte d'auteur" (It's unreadable; we published it at the author's expense) (*Corr.*, 12:290, n. 3).

Proust responds to these attacks on the coherence of *Du côté de chez Swann* in a consistent manner. Whereas these readers object to an apparently homogeneous narrative whose every element has been given equal weight, Proust offers his definition of composition, which is precisely the privileging of certain textual elements over others: his system of *preparations*, the early introduction of characters or themes and their eventual return. Where Proust asserts he has made deliberate choices, then, critics like Souday and Ghéon see lack of method and lack of will; where he has designed a reading on the model of a gradual unveiling, these readers have drawn their conclusions without having reached the end. At the opposite pole of these preemptory judgments is the case of the critic André Beaunier—one of the critics on whom Proust counted the most, according to Philip Kolb (*Corr.*, 12:xxviii). Determined to reserve his judgment for the whole, Beaunier refuses to publish a review until the entire novel has appeared. To Beaunier's refusal—which seems to conform precisely to the principle of Proust's recommended hermeneutical reading—Proust responds, "c'est moi qui vous demande de ne pas attendre cet achèvement si tardif, si incertain" (I myself ask you not to wait for this completion, so far in the future and so uncertain).

Beaunier's refusal, his determination to wait until the entire novel is finished, and finally his death before the appearance of its final volume provide a telling paradigm of the paradox of deferred meaning: a forced alternative between misreading of the part and a complete reading that may never take place. Readings like Souday's and Ghéon's fragmented the so-called indivisible whole just as surely as the publication process had done. Yet Proust's response to Beaunier, the sole critic prepared to put his full reading into practice, is unequivocal: "N'attendez pas que les autres volumes aient paru, parce que 1914 a été mis seulement sur la demande de l'éditeur, pour amorcer une suite" (Don't wait for the other volumes to appear, since 1914 was announced only at the publisher's behest, to get the idea of a sequel going) (*Corr.*, 12:367).

Albertine as Accident

Continuity, wholeness, the enticement to further reading contained within each of the parts: these principles of Proust's creative process were thus reproduced on another level by his first publisher's marketing strategies. Grasset's November 1913 announcement of forthcoming volumes can be thought of as a symbolic bridge between *Du côté de chez Swann* and its unpublished successors, the editorial equivalent of the linking of part to part that Proust called the essential work of composition.[5] But the date 1914, inscribed by Grasset as an *amorce* (at once a beginning and a lure) indicating the direction of the book to come, was the year in which all links were broken: the continuity between the first and second volumes (*À l'Ombre des jeunes filles en fleurs*, now the second volume, appeared in bookstores some five years later); the contract between Proust and his publisher Bernard Grasset; and the basic identity between the three-volume *Recherche* advertised in 1913 and the colossal cycle of novels that emerged after the war—of which Proust said, at the end of his life, that it had only just begun (*Corr.*, 21:56). When *À la recherche du temps perdu* returned to the literary scene in 1919, having nearly doubled in length, its most striking feature was its vast new median section, *Sodome et Gomorrhe*, at the heart of which was the "roman d'Albertine": the story of the hero's love affair with Albertine, one of the young women encountered at the seaside resort of Balbec; of Albertine's sequestered life as a jealously guarded love object; and finally of her flight and accidental death. The episode would soon expand to fill the two volumes most closely associated with Albertine and with Proust's biography, *La Prisonnière* and *Albertine disparue* (*La Fugitive*).[6]

In the initial reception of *Du côté de chez Swann*, Proust encountered a frustrating series of misreadings which he attributed to a failure to perceive the particular, deliberate emphases that served to join this first volume to those to come. But although these readers drew their conclusions from *Swann* alone, the same reproaches of chaos and excess would again arise after everything had appeared. Echoing early assessments of *Swann*, later critics would call Proust's novel disproportionate, disharmonious, and even dysfunctional.[7] The new site of this putative disorder was the "roman d'Albertine."

If Jacques Normand's passing remark that it is just as normal to write twenty volumes as to stop at one or two can be seen as a comment on the text's lack of internal norms—norms that would provide a necessary logic for an ending—a similar assumption of textual normality is behind a later critique, emerging in the 1930s, that the *Recherche* had gone awry somewhere and had failed to develop "normally." But whereas early critics of *Du côté de chez Swann* seemed exasperated by a narrative in which "every single thing carries equal weight" (as Henri Ghéon put it), critics of the postwar *Recherche* were concerned precisely with its *unevenness*—that is, with a perceived irregularity in its pattern of growth and hence in the definitive text. Beginning with the first studies to approach the novel from a genetic point of view, the "roman d'Albertine" has frequently been qualified as an *excrescence*, a genetically distinct outgrowth that remains visibly heterogeneous to the rest of the novel. The perception of disproportion, consistent with the reception of *Swann*, is now expressed (by the figure of the excrescence) in properly organic terms: in terms of the relationship of part to whole. Evoking this frequent interpretation, Jean Milly notes that "tout le cycle d'Albertine . . . a été souvent considéré comme une longue pièce rapportée, une excroissance contingente du récit. Il y a lieu de s'interroger sur cet écart typologique interne et sur le degré d'intégration de ce cycle dans l'ensemble de la *Recherche*" (The entire Albertine cycle . . . has often been considered a lengthy extraneous section, a contingent excrescence of the narrative. This raises the question of an internal typological difference and of the [Albertine] cycle's degree of integration into the *Recherche*) (*Proust dans le texte*, 8). Milly's reference to an "internal typological difference" supports a long-standing view that the median volumes belong to a mode apart. We turn now to a key moment in Proust criticism that saw the first analyses of this "modal incompatibility" (Ellison, *The Reading of Proust*, 111), analyses in which the representation of Albertine as excrescence is fully charged with the normalizing and pathologizing implications of the organic metaphor.

Albert Feuillerat's *Comment Marcel Proust a composé son roman* (1934) was the first study to broach the problem of discontinuity in Proust, as well as the first to identify the First World War as a site of disjunction for the *Recherche* as a whole.[8] It began with the intriguing notion that *À la recherche du temps perdu* comprised two radically different works. One was superimposed upon the other; one was *poetic* and the other *psychological*; they fully cohabited the novel and yet were so distinct from one another in style and tone as to give the impression of a single work produced by two writers collaborating (1). Feuillerat's point of departure was a "change in tone" beginning with *Sodome et Gomorrhe*, which was no longer characterized, he noted, by "cette tonalité unique et si particulière qui faisait le charme de la première version" (this unique and so particular tone that lent the first version its charm) (262). Discerning what he called Proust's "two manners," Feuillerat wondered what stood between the poetically resonant *Du côté de chez Swann* with its "atmosphère de rêve éveillé" (atmosphere of a waking dream) and the dry analytical tone, the baroque digressions of *Sodome et Gomorrhe*. He famously concluded that there were effectively two Prousts: the Proust who had begun writing before the war, "dans la fraîcheur d'une âme presque enfantine" (in the freshness of an almost childlike soul) (262), and a Proust profoundly affected by the war years, "infiniment plus vieux que son âge" (infinitely older than his age), embittered and suspicious of human nature (113). It was this second, misanthropic Proust, he insisted, who was responsible for the Sodom and Gomorrah volumes.

In support of his assertions, which boiled down to the two-Proust theory, Feuillerat proceeded to a partly hypothetical comparison of the three Grasset volumes with the definitive, postwar version (reconstructing the third Grasset volume himself, since it had never been put into galley-proofs). Summing up the post-1914 transformation of the original third volume, he portrayed Proust's successive additions as a *gonflage*, a monstrous swelling of the text itself:

> Ce qui devait être le troisième volume de l'ouvrage a enflé, enflé monstrueusement, *formant dans l'ensemble harmonieux du début deux énormes excroissances*—l'histoire du vice de Charlus et l'histoire d'Albertine—qui, par les dimensions qu'elles ont prises, ont détruit toute possibilité d'équilibre entre les diverses parties, ont même changé la signification profonde de l'œuvre (256, italics mine).

> What would have been the third volume of the work then swelled up, swelled up monstrously, *creating in the original harmonious ensemble two enormous excrescences*—the story of the vice of Charlus and the story of Albertine—which, through the dimensions they took on, destroyed any possibility of equilibrium between the different parts, and even changed the basic meaning of the work as a whole.

Although the destructive character imputed to the added material is obviously linked to the thematic privileging of homosexuality in the additions—Feuillerat calls *excroissances* the narratives of Charlus and Albertine, respective representatives of the world of Sodom and Gomorrah—the manifest logic of Feuillerat's argument is worth following in itself.[9] The added material, he argues, destroyed the original harmony of the first version, growing out of all proportion to the other parts of the novel and obscuring its original framework: three parts of more or less equal length, such as they would have appeared without the outbreak of war. The beginning and end, he concedes—*Du côté de chez Swann* and the final chapter of *Le Temps retrouvé*—remained immutable throughout the additions, but "tout l'entre-deux a été violemment et irrémédiablement disloqué, et sans qu'on puisse trouver la moindre intention constructrice dans la distribution des additions" (the entire in-between has been dislocated, violently and irremediably, without any sign of constructive intention in the distribution of the additions). The implication is that *Du côté de chez Swann*, a "harmonious ensemble," owed its harmony to the coherence and rationality of Proust's original plan—a rationality that would be supplanted by the apparent violence and randomness of the wartime additions.

A similar theory appeared under a different guise a few years later in Robert Vigneron's source study "Genèse de *Swann*" (1937), which marked the beginning of a long critical fascination with Proust's biography. (*Swann* refers here to the *Recherche* as a whole, as consistent with Proust's usage.) It was Vigneron who first suggested that Albertine was modeled after a male love object in Proust's life: his sometime chauffeur and secretary Alfred Agostinelli, the famous "captive" of the Boulevard Haussmann apartment who fled to the South of France in December 1913 and was later killed in a piloting accident.[10] Vigneron affirms with Feuillerat that the 1913 version of the novel, "ce tout organique et complexe" (this complex and organic whole), was guided by a unified, well thought-out aesthetic doctrine (431). But after 1913, the predominance of the aesthetic theme was progressively undone by Proust's interpolations—"monstrous tumors" destroying the integrity of the whole:

> Avec ces additions de toute sorte, la fin de l'œuvre a pris en quelques années des proportions démesurées: les deux volumes annoncés en 1913 pour 1914 sont devenus cinq volumes en 1918 et finiront par en devenir treize. Malheureusement cette croissance de l'œuvre n'a pas été une croissance normale et harmonieuse. *Elle a porté presque uniquement sur certaines portions, qui se sont enflées en tumeurs monstrueuses.* Bien plus, l'ordre des épisodes primitifs a été bouleversé; et les épisodes interpolés ne parviennent pas à s'intégrer à la masse primitive. . . . Il en résulte un inimaginable chaos (529, italics mine).

> With these additions of every kind, the end of the work took on, in the space of a few years, exaggerated proportions: the two volumes announced in 1913 for 1914 became five by 1918 and would eventually become thirteen. Unfortunately, this growth of the

work was not a normal and harmonious growth. *It bore almost exclusively upon certain sections, which swelled up into monstrous tumors.* What's more, the order of the original episodes was completely destroyed; and the interpolated episodes are not well integrated into the original mass of text. . . . The result is an unimaginable chaos.

The aesthetic discourse that is the ostensible context of these arguments can be traced back to Aristotle, but it resonates especially with a particular brand of nineteenth-century organicism: organicism in its evolutionary, developmental sense, which is concerned with creative process as *growth*. If the tumors are supplementary parts that destroy the coherence of the whole just as surely as missing parts would do, the figure of the excrescence suggests a particular concern for the teleology of "normal" creative process. "Tout laissait donc prévoir, en novembre 1913, que *À la recherche du temps perdu* allait se dérouler normalement et harmonieusement, selon . . . le plan dont [Proust] publiait les grandes lignes sans livrer le secret essentiel" (There was every reason to think, in November 1913, that *À la recherche du temps perdu* was going to unfold normally and harmoniously, according to . . . the plan whose general outlines Proust had published, but without giving away its essential secret) (334). Proust's announcement of volumes to come, an editorial formality, functions here as a binding necessity proceeding from within the work itself: deviation from the announcement is tantamount to an aberration in the text's implicitly organic trajectory of growth.

The monstrous excrescence is the figure, then, for an alleged deviation in Proust's writing process, a stylistic and thematic splitting from which his work-in-progress, (posited as) lucid and harmonious before the war, never recovered. The interruption of 1913–14, according to this logic, marks the point at which the *Recherche* went astray, losing contact with the source of inspiration that had assured its original unity—"son unité essentielle d'inspiration et de facture" (its fundamental unity of inspiration and construction) (332). "Genèse de *Swann*" specifically traces this going-astray to a biographical accident. Whereas Feuillerat sought to explain the novel's internal modal differences largely in terms of the historical contingency of the war, Vigneron turns instead to Proust's personal "avant-guerre" (*Corr.*, 14:26), the adversities of 1913–14 that culminated in the death of Alfred Agostinelli. His insistence on the profound unity and impeccable coherence of the 1913 version sets the backdrop for the dramatic focus of "Genèse de *Swann*": Agostinelli's May 30, 1914, piloting accident off the coast of Antibes, the "irreparable and definitive catastrophe" that crystallized all of Proust's sorrows (338).

In a telling reprise of "Genèse de *Swann*" called "Désintégration de Marcel Proust" (1948), the structural function of Agostinelli's tragic accident (for Vigneron's argument) becomes clear: portrayed as a pernicious encounter between text and life, the accident unfolds as biographical *and literary* catastrophe.[11] "Désintégration" distinguishes itself from the earlier essay by a sustained confusion of author and *œuvre* and by a tone of condemnation amply conveyed by its title. Vigneron details Proust's "physiological" and "moral" decline over a period of several years, a decline leading gradually but fatally to the aesthetic disintegration of *À la recherche du temps perdu.* This putative downward spiral begins with Agostinelli's accident—first peripeteia in a series of external circumstances which, along with the "internal adversities" of illness and homosexuality, prevented the novel from appearing in the form originally planned. The process of "disintegration" occurs through Proust's successive additions, represented as a progressive invasion of the self-contained fictional work by elements of raw life. Not only are the post-1914 additions—and in particular the entire episode concerning Albertine—characterized by their direct relation to Proust's life, but they bear the marks, Vigneron suggests, of a too-immediate transposition into fiction.

> Tous les souvenirs de ses vacances à Cabourg avec Agostinelli, de leurs rencontres à Paris, de leur vie Boulevard Haussmann, du départ d'Agostinelli pour la Provence, de sa mort accidentelle, du désespoir sans cesse renaissant et de la jalousie posthume du survivant, Marcel Proust les introduit maintenant à peine transposés dans son œuvre, sans prendre garde qu'il détruit l'ordonnance, l'équilibre, le développement progressif de son plan primitif (526).

All the memories of his vacations in Cabourg with Agostinelli, of their encounters in Paris, of their life together on the Boulevard Haussmann, Agostinelli's departure for Provence, his accidental death, the despair and posthumous jealousy of the surviving lover—Marcel Proust now introduced them into his work under a thin veneer of fiction, paying no heed to the fact that he was destroying the order, the balance, the progressive development of his original plan.

If the introduction of the Albertine episode can be traced directly to Agostinelli's accident (which is indeed the point of "Genèse de *Swann*"), it is doubly accidental: as an unforeseen episode, it also constitutes a creative accident with respect to the rest of the novel. Vigneron's narrative of genesis, which turns into a narrative of organic ruin, borrows from the organicist topos of a simultaneously conceived whole so as to underscore the contingent character of the added episode. In a classically Romantic foundational moment, a "mysterious spark" suddenly crystallizes the material Proust has amassed over the years, and in an "astonishing illumination" his work appears to him. "Il en découvre la matière véritable: les souvenirs de sa vie passée; il en choisit le thème fondamental: l'histoire d'une vocation littéraire; et il en détermine le dessin original: cette composition circulaire qui . . . bouclera si exactement la dernière page sur la première" (he discovers its true material: the memories of his past life; he chooses its fundamental theme: the story of a literary vocation; and he determines its original structure: the circular composition which . . . will bring the last page to close so perfectly upon the first) (319). According to this scenario, the 1913 version corresponded to a kind of blueprint mapped out at the illuminating moment of "conception." Albertine, then, springing from a contingency some years later, does not partake of the original impulse according to which, in organic theory, the work of art is formulated a priori as single and indivisible.

The nexus of ideas and assumptions brought together by the metaphor of the uncontrolled excrescence—literary conception as embryonic, writing as a teleological process, and interruption as inherently dangerous—finds powerful expression, finally, in André Maurois's *À la recherche de Marcel Proust* (1949). In a wildly surrealistic image, Proust's novel becomes the monstrous product of a pregnancy having overrun its term:

> Sur le roman, la guerre avait produit de profonds et surprenants effets. Quand le cours des événements est normal, un livre se détache du créateur au moment où il est publié; le cordon ombilical est coupé; les nouvelles nourritures vont à de nouveaux ouvrages. Mais, parce que la *Recherche du temps perdu* ne pouvait paraître, elle continua de se développer de manière pathologique. Toutes les cellules de ce corps superbe et monstrueux proliférèrent à l'envi. Comme dans une gravure de Piranesi, de puissantes croissances végétales firent éclater les murs de la construction primitive (283).

> The effect of the war on the novel was profound and surprising. When the life of the world is proceeding normally, a book breaks free of its author as soon as it is published; the umbilical cord is cut, and new stimulus produces new works. But because *À la recherche du temps perdu* could not appear, it went on developing in a pathological manner. All the cells of that magnificent and monstrous body proliferated at will. As in one of Piranesi's engravings, growing things and creepers burst through the walls of the original construction (270, English trans.).

Just as publication is posited as the natural telos of the writing process, the 1913 version of the *Recherche* appears here as the moment at which a novel "normally" attains a degree of perfection that is its readiness for publication. That imagined original structure is, of course, a phantom—Proust's Grasset trilogy never appeared as such and no longer exists in an integral form. Like Feuillerat's attempted reconstruction of the Grasset volumes and Vigneron's textual pathology, Maurois's metaphor reifies a transient state of the text by attributing to it the properties of a fully realized natural organism. Reified and idealized, the 1913 version presents a phantasmatic, independent model of unity. The result is this: the invention of Albertine can now be considered the ultimate test of the claims Proust made at the outset, that is, that his simultaneously conceived structure could withstand the vagaries of time itself. The stakes of such a test are bound up with the deepest theoretical questions of organic theory—and can be illuminated by a look at what accident meant to nineteenth-century theoreticians of organicism in art.

Organic Theory and Its Monsters

Analyses such as those I have examined above point toward structuralism in their overriding effort to account for the text as an intelligible *form* whose lines can be clearly drawn. They also reflect a tradition of organicist thinking—equally fascinated by structure—that led to the creation of special categories for the irregular, the accidental, and the monstrous in creative process. In particular, Séailles and his French contemporaries produced a spate of works on the secret of invention during the last two decades of the nineteenth century, writing in the interstices of psychology, philosophy, and aesthetic theory.[12] Their literary organicism borrowed more from biology than its disciplinary prestige. Organistic biology provided precise models and a complete lexicon for plotting the growth of a living organism. Séailles and his cohort represent the work of art, and the literary work par excellence, as following a life trajectory, beginning with the "seed" of its conception and ending in the implicit death of the fixed form. For Séailles, the analogy is unqualified: "L'œuvre d'art, comme l'être vivant, est conçue par un acte d'amour, elle se développe comme lui" (The work of art, like the living being, is conceived by an act of love; it develops in just the same manner) (*Le Génie dans l'art*, 175). Paul Souriau, in his *Théorie de l'invention*, speaks of "embryonic thoughts" formed during a period of gestation (119); Théodule Ribot distinguishes an initial phase in which the ovule awaits fertilization before embarking on its evolution (*L'Essai sur l'imagination créatrice*, 67); and François Paulhan cautions that the seed of invention, whose species is not fixed in advance, might give birth to a novel, a play, or a philosophical treatise, depending on the influence of its milieu (*Psychologie de l'invention*, 104, 107).

Séailles, Souriau, Ribot, and Paulhan articulated their vitalistic theories of invention against the backdrop of the defining polemic that ranged across the disciplines at the end of the nineteenth century: the opposition between the mechanical and the organic as ways of conceiving biological, social, and mental processes.[13] Imbued with the language of this debate are Séailles's characterizations of the work of art as an internally directed being.

"L'œuvre n'est pas un automate, dont les mouvements raides laissent sentir la contrainte d'un ressort extérieur aux pièces qu'il meut; elle est un vivant en qui tout vit, dont le moindre élément frémit et s'agite" (The work of art is not an automaton, whose stiff movements bespeak the constraint of an external lever applied to the parts it moves; it is a living being in which everything is alive, and whose tiniest element quivers and rustles) (*Le Génie dans l'art*, 209). The creative process of the realist writer, on the other hand, consists in creating a "machine" out of separate parts (161); and the antithesis of the living work is one in which "on rapproche savamment des membres morts pour en composer un corps vivant" (one cleverly brings together dead limbs so as to arrange them as a living body) (165). The automaton, the machine, the body assembled from dead members are not yet the monstrous; Séailles proposes them only as negative definitions of the living. But somewhere in between the living organism and its opposite, the machine, lies the possibility of the monster: a living organism gone awry in its development, marked for death but continuing to thrive. The key to the monstrous is in the very stake of the debate between organicism and mechanism—the notion of finality. To what degree was the process of invention determined by a telos, and what role could be ascribed to accident or chance?

If the work of art, once conceived, was bound to develop continuously according to the logic of the living whole, it might also be subject to interruption, deviation, and accident. These eventualities become the object of a special category of invention: the anomalous or monstrous, which occurs most frequently in relation to the literary. Séailles's example of the monstrous clearly suggests that the risk of literary abnormality is linked to the necessary dissociation of conception and execution. In the gap between an initial conception and its realization as *form*, an accident—possibly an unforeseen circumstance in the life of the author—might deflect the fledgling work from its natural, internally determined trajectory. According to Séailles's "law of organic correlation," the various parts of the work of art modify themselves in response to unexpected change so as not to create "a monstrous being" (175). As an example of a literary monstrosity, Séailles cites the case of Goethe's *Faust* with its "two dramas"

(248): the poignant, internal drama of the old philosopher, composed largely of monologues and lacking visible action; and that of the fall and death of Marguerite, a tearful, external drama from which Faust disappears.

Paulhan's *monstre double* offers an equally striking instance of anomalous development. Alongside the categories of evolution (regular systemic growth) and transformation (a complete change of orientation en route), he names a third category, development by deviation. "L'œuvre a évolué, s'est développée, mais il s'est développé en elle des parties parasites, discordantes, qui ont évolué et continué à vivre" (The work has evolved and grown, but there have grown within it parasitical, discordant parts that have evolved and continued to live) (*Psychologie de l'invention*, 135). The hallmark of deviation is *disproportion:* previously marginal elements come to occupy within the whole "une place exagérée, au point que parfois l'œuvre ressemble à un monstre double" (a disproportionate space, sometimes to the point that the work takes on the appearance of a double monster) (136). The *monstre double,* like Séailles's *être monstrueux,* can result from a particular biographical circumstance that makes its way into the fictional work and takes root there. The fictional outgrowth thus sparked by contact between the work-in-progress and life itself then assumes a distinct and independent life of its own. Nothing comes closer to Paulhan's "deviation" than the notion that Proust's novel, having met with the biographical accident of Agostinelli's flight and death, incorporated the material of this real-life drama only to be overwhelmed by its allegedly disproportionate importance.

Ribot, finally, makes a similar tripartite distinction between normal and deviant types of invention.[14] In a chapter on the unifying principle of invention, he classifies the various forms of unity as "organic," "unstable," and "extreme or semi-morbid." This last, anomalous form of unity, which Ribot calls "frankly pathological," is characterized by obsession on the part of the artist, the permutation of the unifying principle into an *idée fixe* (*L'Essai sur l'imagination créatrice,* 72). Although not placed explicitly under the sign of the monstrous, the *idée fixe* shares many features with Paulhan's *monstre double* and Séailles's *être monstrueux.* Parasitical and discordant, it represents a sort of "dédoublement de la conscience" (doubling of consciousness). What was merely suggested by Séailles and Paulhan is fully articulated by Ribot: the extremes of creative process mark a point where the creator is no longer master of his *œuvre.* "L'obsédé est un possédé dont le moi est confisqué au profit de l'idée fixe" (The obsessed [artist] is a possessed man whose self has been confiscated by the *idée fixe*) (73). Here the creature or product of the imagination has become, like Frankenstein's monster, independent, pursuing its own trajectory to the detriment of the creator or to the ruin of the work of art.

Characterizations of the *Recherche* as (genetically) pathological or even monstrous are indebted to the horizon of ideas sketched briefly above. Taken to the logical conclusion so clearly indicated by Ribot, such characterizations imply loss of artistic control—an idea especially evident in representations of Proust's rewriting as an uncontrolled proliferation no longer guided by rational planning. Critical discussions of Albertine's introduction into *À la recherche du temps perdu* continue to turn on this underlying question long after Feuillerat and Vigneron. As another tradition would have it, Proust was thoroughly in control of his creature from beginning to end.

Letters to Agostinelli

Much post-1950 commentary on the invention of Albertine has been articulated as though in response to the notion that the *Recherche* was marked by a genetic trauma traceable to the war years. Alternative morphological models for the postwar shape of the novel suggest a textual coherence that has survived interruptions and absorbed whatever has come into its path. A memorable example is Léon Pierre-Quint's image of a snake swollen with its last meal:

> Toute la guerre de 1914, toute la période de 1914 à sa mort, tant de souvenirs plus anciens qui s'associaient aux moments qu'il continuait de vivre: ses deuils, sa gloire, ses tristes plaisirs sexuels . . . tout cela Proust l'introduisait peu à peu, par ajouts successifs, intercalés à différentes pages, au sein de son ouvrage. Mais celui-ci, tel un serpent, dont la tête et la queue resteraient immobiles

> mais dont le ventre se gonflerait énormément, ne perdait pas sa
> structure initiale (S*tratégie littéraire*, 77–78).

> All throughout the First World War, from 1914 until his death, so
> many older memories joined up with moments in the present: his
> losses, his literary successes, his sad sexual pleasures . . . Proust
> introduced all this into his work, little by little, through succes-
> sive additions inserted on various pages. But the novel, like a
> snake whose head and tail remain unchanged but whose stomach
> swells up enormously, kept its original structure.

Here the text does indeed swell from successive additions, but its
structure is preserved by the immobility of beginning and end
(Proust's insistence on having written simultaneously the first and
last chapters). Contact between text and life is implicitly figured as
nourishment, a metaphor that recalls Proust's own description of
his additions as "cette surnourriture que je leur réinfuse [aux livres]
en vivant, ce qui matériellement se traduit par ces ajoutages" (the
extra nourishment with which I re-infuse [the books] through living, and of which these additions are the material form) (*Corr.*,
18:226; *SL*, 4:75). In a similarly valorized metaphor from the natural
world, Henri Bonnet compared the novel to "une ruche bien conçue
dès le point de départ dont les alvéoles sont aptes à s'accroître d'une
nourriture nouvelle qui les enfle démesurément, mais sans modi-
fier la structure de l'ensemble" (a beehive, well-conceived from the
outset, whose honeycombs tend to grow from new nourishment
that puffs them up enormously but without altering the structure of
the whole) ("La Publication," 2:125). Like Pierre-Quint's serpent,
Bonnet's beehive allows for the eventual introduction of new material without representing it as pernicious excess. Its structure
recalls Proust's use of the terms *severe* and *complex*: severity is the
immutable framework provided by beginning and end, while complexity describes Proust's system of *preparations*—a series of
delayed meanings that constitute an unapparent order beneath
seemingly excessive material (see Chapter 2).

These models of well-conceived, controlled organic process
offer a counterpoint to Maurois's uncanny image of "growing
things and creepers" exceeding the novel's original structure, or
that of the otherwise healthy body riddled with swollen protru-

sions. More pertinent, though, are the genealogical models to which I turn now—critical accounts whose project is to reinscribe Albertine's "lineage" deep within the history of the *Recherche*. Such arguments for the novel's essential continuity minimize the role of contingency in Proust's creative process, lending to the latter sections—those written during and after the war—the necessity of an originary impulse that would predate his personal *avant-guerre* of 1913–14. When Philip Kolb first published Proust's letters to Alfred Agostinelli in his *Lettres retrouvées* (1966), he carefully deconstructed one of the abiding claims of the transposition theory: that Albertine's death in *Albertine disparue* was modeled directly after Agostinelli's real-life accident.[15]

Kolb begins his presentation of the letters by acknowledging what the Albertine episode owed to Proust's own troubled relationship with Agostinelli. In fact, he uncovers a direct conduit between life and text: Proust's literary use of his correspondence with Agostinelli, a technique he borrowed from Chateaubriand. "En se servant de ses propres lettres pour nourrir son œuvre, il ne faisait que suivre un procédé qu'il avait remarqué et approuvé autrefois chez un des auteurs qu'il avait admiré le plus. Au cours de l'été 1908 . . . il note dans un petit carnet: 'Lettres de Chateaubriand à Charlotte utilisées pour *Les Natchez* . . .'" (By using his own letters to nourish his book, he was merely borrowing a technique he had noticed and appreciated in one of the authors he most admired. During the summer of 1908 . . . he noted in a little notebook: "Chateaubriand's letters to Charlotte used in *Les Natchez* . . .") (22). Kolb thus situates Proust's technique within the continuity of a literary tradition, imitation of an admired predecessor; at the same time, he situates Proust's appropriation of Chateaubriand's technique—the moment at which, having read an article on Chateaubriand in *La Revue de Paris*, Proust makes a note of it—within the repertory of ideas and techniques he stored up for later use. Proust's near reproduction of actual correspondence in *Albertine disparue* is thus over-determined by previous texts—*Les Natchez*, and the seminal notebook that contained the lineaments of *À la recherche du temps perdu* (which Kolb later published as *Le Carnet de 1908*). Reattached to Proust's literary heritage, the fictionalized letters now appear at a remove from their biographical context.

Proust insisted, Kolb points out, that his own letters to Agostinelli be returned to him—with "formidable wax seals." Of one letter in particular, which he calls the most precious find of the *Lettres retrouvées*, the letter Proust addressed to Agostinelli on the day of the latter's piloting accident, Kolb asks: "Pourquoi Proust insiste[-t-il] pour qu'Agostinelli lui renvoie cette lettre, comme il lui avait recommandé de faire pour sa précédente let-tre[?] Peut-être est-ce simplement par prudence, afin que ses let-tres ne traînent pas?" (Why does Proust insist that Agostinelli return this letter to him, just as he had done for the preceding let-ter[?] Perhaps it's simply out of prudence, so that his letters don't lie around?") (21). He concludes that Proust, during his correspon-dence with Agostinelli in 1914, had already begun elaborating the episodes concerning Albertine and wished to have the letters back so as to incorporate them into the novel.[16] Kolb goes on to dispute the claim that it was Agostinelli's accident that provided the inspiration for Albertine's:

> Voilà plus d'un quart de siècle, en effet, qu'on va répétant que Proust, en écrivant la mort d'Albertine, s'est inspiré de la mort d'Agostinelli. Et pourtant, nous verrons que ce n'est pas exact. Il est vrai que Proust, après la mort de l'aviateur, a dû remanier cer-tains passages du roman. . . . Néanmoins, ce n'est nullement l'ac-cident d'avion où [Agostinelli] est mort qui a suggéré à l'écrivain l'idée de la mort de son héroïne. Cet épisode—la mort par un acci-dent de cheval—, Proust l'avait conçu bien des années avant la tragédie du 30 mai 1914. La preuve, je la trouve dans une nouvelle d'une importance capitale . . . : "La Fin de la jalousie." Proust avait écrit cette nouvelle vers 1895, et l'a fait publier en 1896 dans *Les Plaisirs et les jours*. Il y esquisse déjà cet incident: le héros, Honoré, meurt d'un accident de cheval, de la même façon qu'Al-bertine. Proust n'avait donc fait que reprendre et élaborer cet épisode, ainsi qu'il a fait en empruntant d'autres éléments de ses écrits de jeunesse, pour son roman (24).

> For a quarter of a century now, critics have been repeating that Proust took his inspiration from Agostinelli's death when he wrote about the death of Albertine. And yet, we shall see that it

is not exactly so. It's true that Proust, after the aviator's death, must have rewritten certain passages of the novel. . . . Nonetheless, it was not Agostinelli's fatal airplane accident that gave Proust the idea for his heroine's death. Proust conceived of this episode—death by an equestrian accident—many years before the tragedy of May 30, 1914. I've found the proof in a short story of capital importance: "La Fin de la jalousie." Proust wrote this story around 1895 and published it in *Les Plaisirs et les jours* in 1896. There he already sketches out the incident: the hero, Honoré, dies in an equestrian accident, just as Albertine does. Proust thus did no more than rework and embellish this episode for his novel, as he did by borrowing other elements from his early writings.

The "quarter of a century" Kolb refers to is the time elapsed since the publication of Vigneron's "Genèse de *Swann*," whose widespread thesis is the unnamed subtext of his argument. Kolb resituates the capital scene of Albertine's death—the moment at which it was conceived—long before the story of Agostinelli and within the history of Proust's *œuvre* (in the larger sense). In the place of contingency he suggests imitation and repetition: in his literary techniques Proust imitates Chateaubriand, in the invention of Albertine's death he repeats his own earlier published writings. In short, Kolb's analysis recontextualizes the Albertine episode within a consistent pattern of creative process that "naturalizes" it as part of the novel's genetic heritage. His focus on the scene of Albertine's accident, the passage most intimately connected to Agostinelli in many readers' minds, is emblematic of his approach. The fictive accident itself, modeled from within Proust's *œuvre*, is no literary or creative accident. Finally, if Vigneron first formulated the problem of discontinuity as a splitting of origins—the prewar version proceeding from the immaculate unity of Proust's "illumination," the Albertine volumes from a separate and unrelated source—he also posited the second source as inextricably tied to Agostinelli's death. Kolb undermines this classic dichotomy between the two sources of inspiration, themselves associated respectively with life (the vital, organically coherent work) and death (the real-life fatality, but also the start of a morbid "disintegration" of the *Recherche*).

Montjouvain

In his classic genetic study *Marcel Proust romancier* (1971), Maurice Bardèche goes a step further. For Bardèche, the introduction of the Albertine episode serves to guarantee the essential continuity of the novel as a whole because it reflects a long-standing authorial intention that preceded the biographical events thought to have inspired it.[17] Conceding that Proust's biography can furnish a point of departure for interpretation, he refuses to recognize in Albertine a direct transposition of Agostinelli—or in the sequence of her flight and death anything but the most superficial resemblance to the events of 1913–14. "Le zèle des commentateurs . . . est peu convaincant," he writes, "lorsqu'ils s'efforcent d'appliquer à Agostinelli les analyses de *La Prisonnière*. Rien ne correspond, sinon des références 'événementielles,' le brusque départ [d'Agostinelli], l'accident, ou des détails qui sont là pour la commémoration mais ne nourrissent pas l'épisode" (The zeal of commentators . . . is not very convincing when they attempt to apply to Agostinelli their analyses of *La Prisonnière*. Nothing corresponds, except references to the events themselves—[Agostinelli's] sudden departure, the accident, and details that have been added to the text in remembrance but do not make up the substance of the episode) (2:230). For if Proust was deeply marked by the crisis of 1913–14 and by the war, this "new Proust" hardly appears in the novel: "contrairement à ce qu'on croit, ce changement a eu peu d'influence sur son livre" (contrary to what is believed, this change had little influence on his book) (2:208). Bardèche's two principal points—that Proust's experience during the war years had little influence on his work, and especially that the Albertine episode is *not* a transposition of the Agostinelli affair—appear to be direct responses to Feuillerat and Vigneron, respectively.[18]

Bardèche's analysis revolves around a key scene of *Sodome et Gomorrhe II* that establishes the dramatic situation of the following two volumes, *La Prisonnière* and *Albertine disparue*. In "Désolation au lever du soleil" (Agony at Sunrise), near the end of *Sodome et Gomorrhe II*, as the narrator prepares to break off his relationship with Albertine, a singular reversal occurs: Albertine reveals her childhood ties to Mademoiselle Vinteuil and her lover, sparking his recollection of the spectacle of sadistic profanation witnessed years before at Montjouvain. The recollection of Mont- jouvain, reviving the narrator's obsessive fears of real or imagined lesbian infidelities, transforms his plans for rupture into a plan to keep Albertine under tight surveillance in his Paris apartment (thereby establishing the situation of *La Prisonnière*). Bardèche seeks to divorce this important passage entirely from biography:

> J'admire les biographes qui voient [dans cette scène] intrépidement une transposition. Ils ont plus d'imagination que moi. Quel aveu d'Agostinelli pouvait empoisonner à jamais l'affection qu'on pou- vait avoir pour lui? . . . Je préfère croire que Proust *suivait en lui- même*, lorsqu'il invente cette scène, *une piste inscrite depuis beaucoup plus longtemps dans son imagination*, depuis le temps où, bien avant de connaître Agostinelli, il inventa la scène de Mont- jouvain pour "préparer" cette péripétie: et, par conséquent, que la "Désolation au lever du jour" n'a aucun rapport, en dépit des apparences, avec Agostinelli. Je vois dans cette scène une péripétie purement imaginaire qui n'a aucun point de contact avec la biogra- phie de Proust, qui a pour fonction d'amener la situation de *La Prisonnière*, et qui a pour origine *la nature hystérique et violente de Proust et une imagination véritablement folle* qui sont en réa- lité un des ressorts secrets de toute son œuvre (2:191, italics mine).

> I admire biographers who intrepidly read into [this scene] a transpo- sition. They have more imagination than I do. What confession from Agostinelli could forever poison the affection Proust bore him? . . . I prefer to believe that Proust, when he invented this scene, *was following within himself a path inscribed in his imagination long before*, ever since the time when—well before meeting Agostinelli—he invented the scene at Montjouvain in order to "pre- pare" this peripeteia; and consequently, that "Agony at Sunrise" has no relationship, despite appearances, with Agostinelli. I see in this scene a purely imaginary episode that has no point of contact with Proust's biography, whose function is to set up the dramatic situa- tion of *La Prisonnière*, and whose origin is to be found in *Proust's violent and hysterical nature and his truly mad imagination*, which are in reality one of the secret sources of his entire work.

Bardèche's argument relies on the assertion of a double continuity. The scene in question is functionally connected to the earlier, pre- war version of the work as the telos of the scene at Montjouvain.

This textual continuity is the result of a deeper continuity, a linear *inscription* ("a path inscribed . . . in his imagination") that finally dissolves into a global *nature* ("hysterical" and "violent"). Substituting the continuity of the imaginary linear path for the disruptive influence of biographical events, Bardèche suggests an unbroken link between the pre- and postwar versions of the *Recherche* and between text and authorial "nature." These connections are consistently organic: the novel in its final form, including late additions, can be traced back to its source as though an *élan vital* had pulsed naturally throughout the work.[19] Untouched by biography ("no point of contact") and having a purely textual function, the passage refers back only to the work itself—the earlier scene from *Du côté de chez Swann*—and, despite its resemblance to life, "springs" directly from Proust's nature and fulfills a long-standing authorial intention. The establishment of textual coherence clearly depends on a rigorous separation between text and the lived time of writing.

To complicate matters, the earlier scene at Montjouvain has taken on a definite importance in critical discussions of structural planning and design. It includes a much-commented addition, introduced sometime between August and November 1913, that ostensibly looks forward to the story of Albertine and to its future diegetic importance.

C'est peut-être d'une impression ressentie aussi auprès de Montjouvain, quelques années plus tard, impression restée obscure alors, qu'est sortie, bien après, l'idée que je me suis faite du sadisme. *On verra plus tard que, pour de tout autres raisons, le souvenir de cette impression devait jouer un rôle important dans ma vie.* C'était par un temps très chaud; mes parents, qui avaient dû s'absenter pour toute la journée, m'avaient dit de rentrer aussi tard que je voudrais; et étant allé jusqu'à la mare de Montjouvain où j'aimais revoir les reflets du toit de tuile, je m'étais étendu à l'ombre et endormi dans les buissons du talus qui domine la maison. . . . Il faisait presque nuit quand je m'éveillai, je voulus me lever, mais je vis Mademoiselle Vinteuil. . . . (*RTP* 1:157, italics mine).

It is perhaps from another impression which I received at Montjouvain, some years later, an impression which at the time remained obscure to me, that there arose, long afterwards, the notion I was to form of sadism. *We shall see, in due course, that for quite other reasons the memory of this impression was to play an important part in my life.* It was during a spell of very hot weather; my parents, who had been obliged to go away for the whole day, had told me that I might stay out as late as I pleased; and having gone as far as the Montjouvain pond, where I enjoyed seeing again the reflection of the tiled roof of the hut, I had lain down in the shade and fallen asleep among the bushes on the steep slope overlooking the house. . . . It was almost dark when I awoke, and I was about to get up and go away, but I saw Mademoiselle Vinteuil. . . . (*Remembrance*, 1:173–74).

The famous scene that follows, where the narrator plays voyeur to Mademoiselle Vinteuil and her lover as they enact a ritual of paternal profanation, was found shocking by at least one contemporary of Proust, Francis Jammes, who suggested that it be struck from *Du côté de chez Swann.* In a letter of September 1919, Proust explained to François Mauriac that it would have been *structurally* damaging to the work as a whole to do so: "Francis Jammes m'avait . . . demandé de supprimer du premier volume . . . un épisode qu'il jugeait choquant. J'aurais voulu pouvoir le satisfaire. Mais j'ai si soigneusement bâti cet ouvrage que cet épisode du premier volume est l'explication de la jalousie de mon jeune héros dans les quatrième et cinquième volumes, de sorte qu'en arrachant la colonne au chapiteau obscène, j'aurais fait tomber la voûte" (Francis Jammes had . . . asked me to omit from the first volume . . . an episode he found shocking. I would have liked to satisfy him. But I've built this work so carefully that the episode from the first volume is the reason for my hero's jealousy in the fourth and fifth volumes, so that by ripping out the pillar with the obscene capital, I would have made the vault cave in) (*Corr.,* 18:404–5). Soon thereafter in a letter to Paul Souday, Proust recalled Souday's criticism of certain "obscure and unnecessary" scenes in *Swann.* The scene at Montjouvain, he continued, is indeed useless in the first volume; "mais son ressouvenir est le soutien des tomes quatre et cinq. . . . En la supprimant, je n'aurais pas changé grand-chose au premier volume; j'aurais, en revanche, par la solidarité des parties, fait tomber deux volumes entiers, dont elle est la pierre angulaire, sur la tête du lecteur" (but its recall is the mainstay of volumes four and five. . . . By suppressing it, I wouldn't have materially altered the first volume; on the other hand, because of the interdependence of the parts, I would have brought two entire volumes of which it is the cornerstone crashing down about the reader's head) (*Corr.*, 18:464; *SL*, 4:98–99). Here and elsewhere, Proust invokes the scene at Montjouvain as proof of the rigorous architecture of the whole. The letter appears to confirm the meaning ordinarily attributed to the prospective reference "We shall see, in due course, that . . . the memory of this impression was to play an important part in my life": through this late addition, Proust appears to draw a direct line leading out from this scene toward the passage known as "Agony at Sunrise," which contains the recollection of Montjouvain.[20]

This reading poses, however, a paradoxical problem of reference. Written onto the manuscript before the publication of *Du côté de chez Swann* in November 1913, the addition is read as though it alluded to an entire episode based on biographical events that had not yet taken place. Antoine Compagnon has called this strange phenomenon a case of precedence of literature over life ("Ce qu'on ne peut plus dire de Proust," 57–59). Claiming that the proleptic addition was meant to refer not to "Agony at Sunrise" but rather to an earlier passage on jealousy ("Danse contre seins," in which the narrator observes Albertine and Andrée dancing together, breasts touching), Compagnon goes on to explain this odd coincidence of the 1913 addition with later developments in the novel by placing Albertine within a lineage of female characters who appear in Proust's drafts long before the flight and death of her putative model Agostinelli. Like Bardèche before him, Compagnon points to the existence of a predecessor to Albertine, Maria, "[qui] remonte à très loin dans la genèse du roman" ([who] goes back very far in the genesis of the novel) and whose traits will resurface in Albertine after 1913. By a process he calls "crystallization," Albertine replaces a series of women appearing in various drafts who disappeared from the final manuscript but who showed Proust's early intention to inflect the narrative toward Gomorrah.

The trope of crystallization, central to Compagnon's analysis, allows for contingency while correcting the purely accidental character once attributed to Albertine's invention. If the details and the importance of the episode are due to a biographical accident, Albertine nonetheless has a history deep within the development of the novel and exists as part of a latent "configuration" waiting to develop. "Les brouillons révèlent des configurations fictionnelles floues auxquelles la vie permet soudain de prendre forme ou de cristalliser. Il y a un matériel romanesque vague, mais l'étincelle manque qui rendra tout cela . . . crédible. Et c'est la vie qui fournit par hasard l'étincelle" (The drafts reveal nebulous fictional configurations which life itself allows suddenly to take form or to crystallize. There is a vague fictional material, but it lacks the spark that will make it all . . . believable. And it's life itself that accidentally furnishes the spark) (58). Compagnon's "matériel romanesque vague" bears a striking resemblance to the "'matière' profuse, mais encore inorganisée" (profuse but as yet unorganized "matter") which, according to Bardèche, haunted Proust's imagination long before the introduction of Albertine and which then took shape with her arrival (*Marcel Proust romancier,* 2:14). The future character of Albertine resides as though in a textual unconscious, ready to break the surface: the vague material waiting for a spark of life, the shadowy figures haunting Proust's imagination, make their way into the definitive version by an obscure but certain teleological force—and then conform to what can be thought of as the text's immanent logic.

Compagnon's effort to uncover what he calls Albertine's "true genesis," her place within a lineage of female characters that would reconnect her to Proust's larger project, typifies critical thinking on the question since Bardèche. Within this logic, the historical and personal contingencies of 1913–14 shape, feed, and inflect the development of the work as a whole, an idea expressed perfectly by Bardèche's metaphor of *détournement* (turning-aside): "Ainsi Albertine qui fait prendre un cours nouveau à l'œuvre de Proust, aussi clairement qu'un rocher ou un promontoir qui détourne le cours d'une rivière . . . n'en est pas moins alimentée . . . par une matière antérieure et étrangère" (Thus Albertine, who changed the direction of Proust's novel, as clearly as a boulder or a promontory that alters the course of a river . . . is nonetheless fed . . . by a material that preexists her and is foreign to her) (2:32). As a linear path long inscribed in Proust's mind or as "unorganized matter" awaiting crystallization, the tentative presence of Albertine in the history of the text or the imagination of the author turns her genesis into the felicitous realization of an order somehow inherent in the text.

Long foreseen in Proust's drafts and yet largely shaped by chance, Albertine continually resists the oppositions between planning and accident, between the assumed autonomy of the fictional work and its perpetual opening onto real-life contingency. Jacques Dubois, in a book chapter tellingly entitled "La Contingente," calls for a reevaluation of Albertine—"tenue longtemps pour un produit quelque peu accidentel d'une dérive de l'imagination et de l'écriture" (long considered a somewhat accidental product of a drifting of the imagination and of writing)—as a site of renewal and transformation for the text's values (*Pour Albertine*, 64). But while the Albertine volumes, traditionally the most marginalized sections of *À la recherche du temps perdu*, have indeed begun to receive more critical attention, the disturbance long associated with her apparently contingent character has far from disappeared. In the following chapter, Proust's insistence on rigor and necessity, as against the arbitrary and contingent, will once again create an interpretive conundrum when his work-in-progress meets with a final interruption.

4 Grasset's Revenge

> One wonders if by some quirk of history this is to
> be Grasset's editorial revenge, in the form of a com-
> mercial coup, for losing Proust to Gallimard.
> —Christie McDonald, *The Proustian Fabric*

Some nine months before his death, Proust announced
to his publisher Gaston Gallimard that the *Recherche* had
scarcely begun. "J'ai tant de livres à vous offrir qui, si je meurs
avant," he wrote in February 1922, "ne paraîtront jamais (*À la
recherche du temps perdu* commence à peine)" (I have so many
books to offer you which, if I die before then, will never appear—
À la recherche du temps perdu has scarcely begun) (*Corr.*, 21:56).
Proust's eleventh-hour remark to Gallimard clearly indicates a
state of affairs that has relatively recently come to the attention of
the public: *À la recherche du temps perdu* is an unfinished work.
The announcement of future volumes that appeared in *La Nouvelle Revue Française* just days after Proust's death bears witness
not just to the novel's incompletion, but to the stunning extent of
it. "In press: *Sodome et Gomorrhe III. La Prisonnière; Albertine
disparue.* Forthcoming: *Sodome et Gomorrhe* in several volumes
(*suite*); *Le Temps retrouvé* (conclusion)" (see Chapter 1). This
barely posthumous announcement of several volumes to come—
volumes that would never see the light of day—illustrates beautifully what Proust called elsewhere *announcing in doubt.* Just
before his death he wrote to Gallimard, referring to *La Prisonnière*

and *Albertine disparue,* "Si vous désirez, *dans le doute,* annoncer mes deux volumes suivants pour 1923, bien volontiers cher ami. Mais . . . je ne peux prendre aucun engagement" (If you wish to announce, *in doubt,* my next two volumes for 1923, go right ahead, dear friend. But . . . I cannot make any promises). He concluded by making his ritual connection between the practice of announcing and the threat of death: "En ce moment je vais un peu mieux cela me permet de me remettre au travail. Mais qui sait ce que demain me réserve. Si donc m'annoncer, c'est me promettre, non, ne m'annoncez pas" (Being slightly less ill at the moment, I can get down to work. But who knows what tomorrow has in store. Therefore, if to announce my books means committing me, then, no, don't announce them) (*Corr.,* 21:331; *SL,* 4:394, first translation modified). The final announcement ostensibly signifies an engagement on the part of the Nouvelle Revue Française to produce these last, vaguely designated volumes; but it is a promise whose real guarantor has disappeared, and it has since come to be read as a kind of text itself, a text that preserves the "letter" of Proust's intention for future generations of critics.[1]

Proust's long-anticipated disappearance in 1922 seems to have left his Nouvelle Revue Française editors in a quandary. Their unexplained advertisement of several more volumes in the *Sodome et Gomorrhe* series suggests that they expected to discover the corresponding notebooks among his manuscripts and were then disappointed. Proust had indicated just such an expansion in a letter to Gallimard at the beginning of the year, referring to an eventual "Sodome IV," "Sodome V," and "Sodome VI" (*Corr.,* 21:39; *SL,* 4:290). But if toward the end of his life Proust once again intervened in every imaginable material detail of the publication process—dates of appearance, intervals between volumes, pagination, font size, the number of lines to a page, and down to the colored ribbon in which the text was wrapped—his sudden silence was all the more remarkable now. In 1986, sixty-four years after his death, when the corrected typescript of *Albertine disparue* was discovered among the papers of Suzy Mante-Proust, its unearthing was followed by a multiplication of critical voices that seemed to compensate for the absence of his once active, explicit editorial voice. In the intense interpretive effort set off by the rediscovery of the typescript, the slimmest traces of intention have become interpretable: the soiled envelope on which Proust scrawled his last words, the crossed-out note ending in anacoluthon, the "relative assurance" of the hand that formulated the incipit to *Albertine disparue* ("Ici commence *Albertine disparue*, suite du roman précédent *La Prisonnière*") (Here begins *Albertine disparue*, sequel to the preceding novel *La Prisonnière*).[2] The story of the *Recherche* after the disappearance of its author—and of the signposts he continually offered editors and readers—is fraught with disputes over the smallest of the indications Proust left behind.

The First Posthumous Editions: 1923–27

Without a doubt, the first editors of the posthumous volumes—the Nouvelle Revue Française, with Marcel's brother Robert Proust at the helm—were intent on keeping their engagement to the reading public.[3] Respecting the spirit, if not the letter, of its December 1, 1922, insert announcing the complete publication of *À la recherche du temps perdu*, the Nouvelle Revue Française went on to publish *La Prisonnière*, *Albertine disparue*, and *Le Temps retrouvé* from 1923 to 1927, with no indication to readers that the novel was incomplete. Proust had died in the midst of an extensive revision: having finished the laborious correction of the copy-proofs for *La Prisonnière*, he had moved on to its sequel, *Albertine disparue*; his death on November 18 had followed an arduous night of work (see Tadié, *Marcel Proust*, 775–79). As though to confirm the impression of completion given by the announcement, the Nouvelle Revue Française published a series of photographs of Proust's heavily corrected manuscript in its January 1923 "Hommage à Marcel Proust." All four photographs are of Notebook XX, the last of Proust's handwritten notebooks; one depicts its label, with the words "twentieth and last" clearly visible in the author's handwriting. Most striking is the commentary that accompanies a photograph of the final page of Notebook XX: "LA DERNIERE PAGE DU MANUSCRIT portant la mention *Fin* de la main de Proust" (the final page of the manuscript, bearing the notation *End* in Proust's hand) (*Nouvelle Revue Française* 112, January 1, 1923). The journal thus appeared to present to its readers, in an issue fittingly dedicated to the memory of Marcel Proust, incontrovertible evidence that the end of Proust's life was concomitant with the completion of his *œuvre*—or even synonymous with it, since the photographs of the manuscript alternate with photos of the author.

Another year would pass before the Nouvelle Revue Française began publication of the final series of notebooks, but in the meantime a new announcement appeared, revising and displacing the first: "In press: *La Prisonnière.* Sodome et Gomorrhe III. In preparation: *Albertine disparue.* Sodome et Gomorrhe (*suite*). *Le Temps retrouvé*" (*Nouvelle Revue Française* 116, May 1, 1923; back cover). The subtitle Proust had assigned to *La Prisonnière* and *Albertine disparue* together, *Sodome et Gomorrhe III*, has been shifted to *La Prisonnière* alone; and under a new rubric, "In preparation," *Albertine disparue* has absorbed the originally announced sequel to *Sodome et Gomorrhe*, the "several volumes" that now evaporate. Did readers of *La Nouvelle Revue Française* notice this disappearance, the telescoping of the anticipated "several" into one? While the new advertisement follows the pattern typical of earlier announcements made during Proust's lifetime—a pattern of revision and displacement, in which each new announcement reflects an unforeseen development in the work—here, for the first time, expansion is replaced by compression. Unlike the earlier announcements that recorded a characteristic movement of proliferation, this posthumous announcement with its curtailment of volumes records the editorial cover-up of a lacuna, indicating for the careful reader the novel's state of incompletion.

Remarkably, *Albertine disparue* was still presented as being "in preparation" as late as September 1924, nearly two years after the first posthumous announcement. As publication of the series neared completion and announcements for the complete works of Marcel Proust appeared less and less frequently in *La Nouvelle Revue Française,* the subtitle erroneously apposed to *Albertine disparue*—"*Sodome et Gomorrhe,* suite"—disappeared: by October 1925, it was nowhere to be found. One might conjecture that the Nouvelle Revue Française, imagining that enough time had passed, hoped their readers had forgotten about the announcement of an expanded *Sodome et Gomorrhe* series. But implicit in their continuing presentation of the *Recherche* was the promise of a coherent series, and it is the attempt to fulfill this promise that lies behind the aptly titled rubric "Sous préparation." The preparation of Proust's final notebooks after his death can be described as an effort to eliminate incoherence on several levels: certainly, by correcting particular incoherencies in the text, repetitions and inconsistencies which Proust had no time to revise; but also by restoring to *Albertine disparue* the material he had cut, so as to safeguard its narrative ties with *Le Temps retrouvé*.[4] While most minor incoherencies were normalized—the resurrection of characters whose death occurs in an earlier volume, traces of multiple proper names—many signs of incompletion subsisted after publication. Paradoxically, these signs may have worked to reassure readers that Proust was in the ultimate stages of revision at the time of his death, and that his editors had before them a fundamentally coherent manuscript that called for only cosmetic changes. Whatever degree of incompletion was evident to the readers of these volumes, the promise of coherence implied by the just posthumous announcement, and by the subsequent inclusion of *À la recherche du temps perdu* in a collection of complete works, was fulfilled by the Nouvelle Revue Française edition. The final volumes appeared from 1923 to 1927, their narrative continuity intact, each part carefully joined to the next—precisely what Proust had called the essential and most difficult part of composition.

Death as Editor: Grasset's Albertine disparue

The modern era of posthumous editing began in 1987, as Proust's manuscripts fell into the public domain. Readers were greeted by a flurry of new editions, each with its own editorial philosophy: Flammarion, Bouquins-Laffont, la Pléiade. One name in particular was strangely familiar: Grasset Editions, whom Proust left for Gallimard in 1916, reappeared with a separate edition of *Albertine disparue*, the penultimate volume of the *Recherche*, based on the newly rediscovered typescript corrected by Proust just before his death—a document unknown to the other publishing houses. This slim volume, which dispenses with some 250 typescript pages in one sweeping deletion, would have an iconoclastic effect, putting into question the canonicity of generations of previous posthumous editions. It advances the argument that Robert Proust and the Nouvelle Revue Française, ignoring Proust's last corrected document, created a doctored, unauthorized version of *Albertine disparue* from the fragments Proust left behind—in order to preserve narrative coherence and hence the illusion of a completed work. The editors of the Grasset volume, Nathalie Mauriac and Étienne Wolff, proceed on radically different assumptions about the task of the editor. What governs this edition is the philosophy of final intentions, long the basis for traditional textual criticism. A "finally intended" text, according to Jerome McGann in his *Critique of Modern Textual Criticism*, is based on the author's last draft and theoretically appears as the author wanted it to read. The author's necessarily coherent intentions are the sole locus of literary authority. The finally intended text "corresponds to the 'lost original' which the textual critics of classical works sought to reconstruct by recension. Both are 'ideal texts'—that is to say they do not exist in fact—but in each case the critics . . . work toward their ideal text by a process of recension that aims to approximate the Ideal as closely as possible" (56). The rediscovered typescript is an actual text, but it functions like an imaginary "lost original"; indeed, that it was in fact lost for some fifty years—between the death of Robert Proust and that of his daughter Suzy—intensifies its *aura* as an original draft bearing the final indications of Marcel Proust.[5]

Grasset's *Albertine disparue* produced something of an event in the world of Proust criticism, detonating a lengthy debate over the status of Proust's final text. A round of polemical articles on the subject appeared in scholarly journals and in the French and Italian press between 1987 and 1998. The stakes of this debate, simply put, have to do with how we are now to read *À la recherche du temps perdu:* if this drastically abridged version of *Albertine disparue* was indeed the beginning of a complete restructuring of the final volumes of the *Recherche,* then Proust left his novel without an ending. This is essentially the hypothesis of the Grasset editors, who maintain that although Proust was interrupted in his revisions, the rediscovered typescript is the definitive version of *Albertine disparue.* As sole authoritative text, it displaces its canonical predecessors and leaves the end of the novel in pieces.

Three other possibilities allow us to take account of Proust's ultimate revisions while continuing to read the *Recherche* with its traditional narrative coherence undisturbed. Jean Milly emphasizes the provisional character of the corrected text and accords it the status of a pre-text—an authentic but nondefinitive draft; his "integral" edition of *Albertine disparue*, which I discuss further on, puts this philosophy into effect. Another hypothesis, which created quite a stir in the press on both sides of the Alps, would permit us to go on reading the *Recherche* in good conscience without changing anything. According to this hypothesis, popularized by Giovanni Macchia, the shortened version of *Albertine disparue* was the preparation of an excerpt Proust had promised to the literary journal *Les Œuvres libres*—a promise that gave rise to a bitter dispute with Gaston Gallimard and Jacques Rivière, who considered publication of excerpts in *Les Œuvres libres* to be harmful to their own impending publication of the volume (see Chapter 1).[6] Finally, the editor of the Italian translation *Albertine scomparsa*, Alberto Beretta Anguissola, proposes in his notice to the volume a fascinating possible destination for the pages Proust eliminated from *Albertine disparue*. Placed after the trip to Venice and the forgetting of Albertine (in a hypothetical "Sodome et Gomorrhe IV"), they would confirm the "intermittencies of the heart" pattern established much earlier by the grandmother's death, alternating oblivion with intermittent, explosive grief.[7]

The claim to exclusive authority represented by the Grasset edition is articulated largely through a sustained critique of the original Nouvelle Revue Française edition and its avatars—notably, the 1989 Pléiade edition of *Albertine disparue*. Nathalie Mauriac Dyer's "Les Mirages du double: *Albertine disparue* selon la Pléiade" unfolds as a powerful illustration of the ideology of final intentions. The traditional method for establishing a "finally intended" text, according to McGann, is to find and eliminate the errors that have inevitably corrupted the text in the process of its transmission, "by revealing the history of their emergence" (*A Critique of Modern Textual Criticism*, 15). The classical method, McGann specifies, "sought to 'clear the text' of its corruptions and, thereby, to produce (or approximate)—by subtraction, as it were—the lost original document, the 'authoritative text.'" The privilege of the lost original document resides in its supposed anteriority to editorial intervention, an intervention conceived as analogous to the work of classical scribes. "Les Mirages du double" sets out to establish the authority of the Grasset edition by revealing the history of error in the transmission of *Albertine disparue* since 1922. This history of error revolves around the circulation of a carbon double in place of the typescript corrected by Proust, an allegedly contaminated copy—the *Albertine disparue* restored by the Nouvelle Revue Française—that goes on to serve as a model for future editors of the *Recherche*. Within the perspective of the classical method, the infamous double can be thought of as a bastard in the line of textual descent that textual critics call, tellingly, an ancestral series (McGann, 39). Thus the Pléiade editors, who place their edition in the "direct filiation" of the 1925 edition ("Mirages," 119), assure by this lineage not the text's authenticity, but the reproduction of the errors of the Nouvelle Revue Française.

Once the illegitimacy of the double is proved, the rediscovered typescript can claim its legitimate place as the exact, unmediated representation of Proust's final intentions. Indeed, this exactitude is presented as the defining characteristic of the Grasset edition: "*Albertine disparue*, dernier tome d'*À la recherche du temps perdu* auquel Marcel Proust ait travaillé, est ici . . . intégralement publié dans l'état exact où il en laissa, à sa mort le 18 novembre 1922, la dactylographie partiellement corrigée" (*Albertine disparue*, the last volume of *À la recherche du temps perdu* on which Marcel Proust worked, is here . . . integrally published in the exact state in which he left its partially corrected typescript at his death on November 18, 1922) (*Albertine disparue* [Grasset], 11). The true original beneath appearances, then—the "authentic face" of *Albertine disparue*, distinct from the "original physiognomy" re-created by the Pléiade—is simply the corrected typescript untouched by posthumous editors: edited, that is, by death alone.[8]

Proust's Deletions

Jean Milly, comparing the rediscovered text to the inhabitants of Pompeii buried beneath the ashes of Mount Vesuvius, counters that the typescript is definitive only "au sens où la mort peut nous figer dans une dernière posture vivante" (in the way that death can freeze us in a final living pose) ("Retitrage," 155). His "integral" edition of *Albertine disparue,* originally published in 1992 by Champion-Slatkine and reedited in 2003 by Flammarion, thus sets itself in opposition to the Grasset editors' claim that there is now one legitimate text.[9] For Milly the two versions, long and short, coexist and are both authentic. Following this logic, the Flammarion edition symbolically reproduces Proust's ultimate revisions to *Albertine disparue* without putting them into effect: additions appear within brackets, while deletions are indicated by means of a vertical bar running alongside the text. Coded and marked but not obscured, they are left to function within a narrative continuity. It is this narrative intactness, the preservation of *readability,* that Milly presents as the principal advantage of his edition. "La présentation du texte est . . . *intégrale,* lisible de bout en bout comme l'étaient les éditions anciennes, mais avec quelques artifices très simples qui font apparaître, sans effort de lecture nouveau, les différentes couches chronologiques" (The presentation of the text is . . . *integral,* readable from one end to the other like the old editions, but with a few simple artifices that make visible, with no new effort required of the reader, the different chronological stages) (*Albertine disparue* [Flammarion], 10, Milly's italics). The term *integral,* which the Grasset editors also use to qualify their edition, takes on quite another meaning here. *Integrality* is synonymous here with linear readability, that is, the restoration of a satisfying narrative logic to *Albertine disparue*—the very objective of the original Nouvelle Revue Française edition. But Milly's version of readability is uniquely historicized, combining the idea of a continuous, linear reading with a diachronic reading of the text's genetic development—visible in the typographical symbols that differentiate the various stages of revision.

Based on the principle of *mise-en-réserve,* or setting-aside, the Flammarion edition represents Proust's corrections as provisional and contingent, that is, as the expression of what Elyane Dezon-Jones has aptly called "arrested intentions" ("Éditer Proust," 52). Milly reproduces the note by which Proust marked his most significant deletion:[10] "De 648 à 898, rien, j'ai tout ôté. Donc nous sautons de 648 au chapitre deux . . ." (From 648 to 898, nothing, I removed everything. Thus we skip from 648 to chapter two . . .). The terms *ôter* (to remove) and *sauter* (to skip), he affirms, indicate that the crossed-out passages were to be set aside for later use. "Les barres obliques qui raient les pages supprimées ne sont pas des barres d'annulation, mais comme ce n'est pas rare chez Proust, l'indication que ces passages sont, ou doivent être, repris ailleurs" (The horizontal lines that bar the suppressed pages are not lines of annulment, but rather, as is often the case with Proust, a sign that these passages are to be inserted elsewhere) ("Retitrage," 155). Like the horizontal bar that separates signifier from signified in Lacan's figure representing the Saussurean linguistic sign ("L'instance de la lettre," 253), the Proustian bar is conceived here as a mark of separation and of repression: it separates passages from the continuous text, but in such a way that the same material will inevitably reappear elsewhere.

Proust's long-standing practice, in fact, was to leave crossed-out material legible by means of a single line running through it, and even to leave fully crossed-out pages in their place in the manuscript or typescript (Douglas Alden even remarked that an earlier version of the narrative was left fully visible in the crossed-out, typed-over text of the Grasset proofs [*Marcel Proust's Grasset Proofs*, 13]). But if the verbs *to remove* and *to skip* do not indicate destruction, if the line that bars them from the text is a bar of repression rather than suppression, the question remains as to how Proust's markings alter the meaning of *Albertine disparue.* The term that appears most frequently to describe the combined effect of Proust's additions and deletions is *condensation,* a term that indicates, beyond the "total economy" which governed his composition (*Corr.*, 12:190), an *economy of meaning* at work in his revisions.

Although Proust's final revisions are frequently construed as a destructive or inexplicable act—as mutilation, dismemberment, even as *massacre* (Macchia, *L'Ange de la nuit,* 248)—this implied violence is largely compensated by a willingness to identify a new order of meaning behind Proust's apparently destructive revisions. In their repeated use of the term *condensation,* Proust's editors do not explicitly make reference to the Freudian notion of *Verdich-*

tung, which appears as one of the key elements of the dream-work. But the analogy is compelling: in the context of *Albertine disparue*, Proust's condensation functions remarkably like the process Freud defined under the same name. According to Freud's formulation, condensation is a process of abridgment by means of which a laconic expression replaces lengthier psychic material, which is thereby censored (*The Interpretation of Dreams*, 269–72). Proust's single addition to the scene of Albertine's death is now familiar to us. The telegram announcing her death, in the canonical editions, tells us simply that Albertine was the victim of an equestrian accident; in the Grasset edition, the telegram specifies the place of her death, the banks of the Vivonne River ("une promenade qu'elle faisait au bord de la Vivonne"). In a second addition, Proust's narrator extrapolates from the meaning of the first: "Ces mots: 'au bord de la Vivonne,' ajoutaient quelque chose de plus atroce à mon désespoir. Car cette coïncidence qu'elle m'eût dit dans le petit tram qu'elle était amie de Mademoiselle Vinteuil, et que l'endroit . . . où elle avait trouvé la mort fût le voisinage de Montjouvain, cette coïncidence ne pouvait être fortuite" (Those words: "on the banks of the Vivonne," added an atrocious note to my despair. For the coincidence of these two things—Albertine having told me in the tram that she was a friend of Mademoiselle Vinteuil, and the fact that she met with her death in the vicinity of Montjouvain—this coincidence could hardly be fortuitous) (*Albertine disparue* [Grasset], 112). With this addition and its spontaneous interpretation by the narrator, over 250 pages of text disappear: the endless production of hypotheses relative to Albertine's sexual past, the narrator's investigative madness, give way to the hastened arrival of the final stage of Albertine's disappearance, oblivion.

If in the dream-work two different elements can be fused together to form a new unity, here Proust's addition, by placing Albertine's death in the vicinity of Montjouvain, functions by joining the event of her death to the (subjective) confirmation of her lesbianism. The dream-work lights upon an ambiguous word in which disparate meanings can be combined. Just so, the phrase *au bord de la Vivonne*, according to the Grasset editors, superimposes several meanings: the association of Albertine with water recalls her first appearance in *À l'Ombre des jeunes filles en fleurs,* where she emerges against the backdrop of the sea in Balbec; it abolishes the absolute demarcation between the two apparently divergent paths, Guermantes and Méséglise, by indicating the proximity of the Vivonne River (Guermantes) to Montjouvain (Méséglise), anticipating their reconciliation in *Le Temps retrouvé;* and, most important, it provides the narrator with what I will call metonymical "proof" of Albertine's lesbianism—she was riding on the banks of the Vivonne, therefore near to Montjouvain, therefore near to Mademoiselle Vinteuil and her lover.

The new dénouement suggested by Proust's revisions effectively presents a coherent solution to the omitted material, just as Freudian condensation creates a new logic in place of the material omitted by the dream-censorship. Indeed, Jean Milly designates the pages marked for omission—the equivalent of two entire manuscript notebooks—as the only cut material that could not be recycled in an ulterior volume ("Faut-il?" 17). Significantly, what the addition puts an end to is the interminable work of mourning and morbid jealousy, so often qualified as "excessive," both structurally and affectively. The work of condensation, in this light, is doubly economical, since the curtailment of mourning is synonymous with narrative concision. The figure of condensation reconfigures Proust's revisions within a coherent, though occulted, strategy of meaning. It suggests that they are not random debris left over from his death but rather fragments of a meaningful whole whose coherence can be restored only through an interpretive process. These putatively meaningful, but effectively destructive, revisions now comprise the principal problem facing editors of the posthumous volumes: how to produce a readable edition while taking account of Proust's changes to *Albertine disparue,* their interpretation definitively in suspense.[11]

The Task of the Editor

Proust's wish to publish *Du côté de chez Swann* in the form of "something normal and accessible," as he put it in his correspondence with Grasset (*Corr.,* 12:100), was contradicted by an equally important imperative: to end the volume as late as possible, so that the reader would be well advanced in the narrative before arriving at the rupture of a volume ending and an interval. Accessibility and readability, the two principal attributes Proust sought in the individual volume, were continually at odds with one another. Whereas the volume could be made accessible only by setting the right price and agreeing to a reasonable number of pages, *readability* implied respect of the particular internal logic of the narrative. The work of reading, especially as Proust articulated it during the publication of *Swann*, was neither linear nor simple. It demanded of the reader a continual turn backward, the suspension of conclusions, and the ability to hold in mind a totality over the duration of the reading process. His system of *preparations*, which delayed comprehension through several volumes, defined reading as repetition and deception—since the return of a character or an episode was often the correction of a misleading first impression (see Chapter 1).

If I recall these concepts in the context of posthumous editing, it is because Proust's formulations of editorial intervention (in the simplest sense of a mediation between writing and being read) suggest two paradoxical editorial modes that characterize the competing editions of *Albertine disparue* under discussion. These modes can be thought of as transparency and obstacle, respectively.[12] By the time Grasset assumed publication of *Swann*, Proust had arrived at the idea that the publisher's task was to give the manuscript an accessible material form without interposing his will between text and reader—in other words, without reading the manuscript (see Chapter 2). Editorial reading, once seen by Proust as the sine qua non of the publication process, had taken on the shape of an obstacle. His insistence on publishing at his own expense had become shorthand for reducing editorial interference to a minimum. But although Grasset indeed tended toward editorial transparency, Proust was especially aware of the instances in which his publisher willfully acted upon the text in obstacle mode—the shortening of *Du côté de chez Swann* being the salient example of such intervention. The fact that a tension between transparency and obstacle inhered in any editorial process seemed to become clearer to Proust in his relationship with Gallimard.[13]

The inevitable tension between these two modes is especially apparent in the respective approaches to posthumous editing represented by the Grasset and Flammarion editions of *Albertine disparue.* The materiality of editorial intervention in Milly's edition epitomizes the mode of the obstacle. The presence of the editor in the text, far from being disguised, is made palpable by typographical symbols that not only demarcate Proust's additions and deletions, but also mark instances of editorial decision with respect to their status. At the antipodes of this frank mediation, the Grasset edition aims for an illuminating transparency that would restitute, as though in the form of a transcript, Proust's actual text to the reader—and behind it the transcendental authority of final intentions: "l'état ultime du texte d'*Albertine disparue* et, dans la mesure du possible, *la dactylographie retrouvée elle-même*" (the final state of *Albertine disparue* and, insofar as possible, *the rediscovered typescript itself*) (*Albertine disparue* [Grasset], 15, italics mine). The actual document in its immediacy appears, in fact, in photographic form in the Grasset edition. Four facsimiles reproduce not only Proust's major additions and deletions, but pages where beginnings and ends are clearly marked ("Ici commence *Albertine disparue*"; "Fin du premier chapitre"; "Fin d'*Albertine disparue*"). As Mauriac Dyer herself has argued, the Nouvelle Revue Française sought to give an impression of the work's completion by repeatedly reproducing Proust's manuscript notation of the word *fin*; these photographs, in a like manner, insist on the finality of the text in their reproduction of the deathbed indications of chapter and volume endings in Proust's wavering hand.

Thus, what is conceived as a set of accidental features by Milly—Proust's precipitous revisions in the face of impending death—is presented by the Grasset edition as the necessary form of *Albertine disparue,* whose every letter must be respected. Proust's own notion of necessity in form was inextricably tied to his wariness of the power of editing: he resisted what he called its arbitrary decisions as so many violations of an ideal form that could not be altered without loss of meaning (see Chapter 2). Proust's notion of necessary form rests on the characteristically Romantic assumption that in the work of genius, language itself is not accidental but is the unique expression of a transcendent design; the creator is merely the locus of "ces pensées qui élisent elles-mêmes à tout moment, fabriquent et retouchent la forme nécessaire et unique où elles vont s'incarner" (those thoughts that, by themselves, constantly elect, construct, and revise the necessary and unique form that will incarnate them).[14] The necessity of form reappears in the celebrated topos of the inner book, where Proust's narrator assimilates writing to translation. The "essential, the only true book" is not a product of invention but is contained within us, waiting for expression ("un grand écrivain n'a pas . . . à l'inventer . . . mais à le traduire. Le devoir et la tâche d'un écrivain sont ceux d'un traducteur") (the essential, the only true book . . . does not have to be "invented" by a great writer . . . [but] translated by him. The function and the task of a writer are those of a translator) (*RTP,* 4:469; *Remembrance,* 3:926). The material form of the literary work is, then, necessary and unique because it approximates or corresponds to the inner book—"le seul que nous ait dicté la réalité, le seul dont l'"impression' ait été faite en nous par la réalité même. De quelque idée laissée en nous par la vie qu'il s'agisse, *sa figure matérielle,* trace de l'impression qu'elle nous a faite, est encore *le gage de sa vérité nécessaire*" (the only one which has been dictated to us by reality, the only one of which the "impression" has been printed in us by reality itself. When an idea—an idea of any kind—is left in us by life, *its material pattern,* the outline of the impression that it made upon us, remains behind as *the token of its necessary truth*) (*RTP,* 4:458; *Remembrance,* 3:913–14, italics mine). Proust's habitual distinction between the *œuvre réelle* and its published form reaffirms this necessity of correspondence between mode of expression and the transcendental signified. Ideally, the work of editing would continue the task of perfect transcription begun by the writing project, matching the inner book with its necessary outer form.

Grasset's *Albertine disparue* is imbued with the same Romantic ideology. Reproducing Proust's final text in its exactitude, it purports to give unmediated access to a stable, autonomous *œuvre* inhabiting the outer form but distinct from it. Thus, even as the Grasset editors acknowledge the role of contingency in the creation of *Albertine disparue,* they nonetheless present this text as the incomparable expression of Proust's will to achieve greater unity through his changes and additions. The most striking expression of this assumption can be found in the conscious repetition of Proust's metaphor of "illumination." Recalling his description of Ruskin's epigraph to *Sesame and Lilies* as a "rayon supplémentaire qui . . . illumine rétrospectivement tout ce qui a précédé" (supplementary ray of light that . . . retrospectively illuminates whatever has preceded it), Mauriac Dyer refers to Proust's final addition to the typescript as a "fulgurante illumination" that brings into relief the unity of the *Recherche* as a whole (*Albertine disparue* [Grasset], 15). The addition, she adds, is "retrospectively necessary." The phrase inevitably evokes a significant theoretical passage of *La Prisonnière* which Jean-Yves Tadié has qualified as the definition of Proust's *art poétique* (*Marcel Proust*, 760). Proust argues in this passage that the great incomplete works of the nineteenth century—those of Balzac, Michelet, or even Wagner—were unified retroactively by a final addition or stroke, "le dernier et le plus sublime" (the last and the most sublime). If this oblique reference to Proust's discussion of retroactive unity in *La Prisonnière* encourages us to see in his final addition the kind of unifying stroke he calls *sublime*, it also points toward the aesthetic alternative at issue in the same discussion: an alternative between formal and organic unity. Proust concludes his passage on the great unfinished works of the nineteenth century in favor of a unity that is at once "ulterior" and "vital." "Unité ultérieure, non factice . . . Non factice, peut-être même plus réelle d'être ultérieure, d'être née d'un moment d'enthousiasme où elle est découverte entre des morceaux qui n'ont plus qu'à se rejoindre, unité qui s'ignorait, donc vitale et non logique" (An ulterior unity, but not a factitious one . . . Not factitious, perhaps indeed all the more real for being ulterior, for being born of a moment of enthusiasm when it is discovered to exist among fragments which need only to be joined together; a unity that was unaware of itself, hence vital and not logical) (*RTP*, 3:667; *Remembrance*, 3:158).[15] The opposition developed here between vital and logical unity is precisely what drives the polemic between the two editions, each one representing not only an editorial modality but a way of conceiving literary coherence.

The process of *montage* at work in the Flammarion edition suggests an editorial philosophy that could not be further removed from the philosophy of genius. Based on the assumption that the typescript represents an arbitrarily arrested moment of the creative process, Milly's edition proposes the artificial reconstruction of a whole in place of the fragmented text Proust left behind. The aim of *montage*—a term which Milly adopts with reference to Proust's own method of "démontage" and "remontage" ("Faut-il?" 29)—is to construct a totality that never existed as such, by submitting all available documents to the reader's judgment: "une édition intégrale . . . qui expose toutes les données du problème et reproduit tout ce que nous possédons d'authentique" (an integral edition . . . that exposes all the factors of the problem and reproduces everything authentic in our possession) ("Faut-il?" 25). The Flammarion edition thus presents *Albertine disparue* as perpetually under construction, an idea expressed very precisely by the repetition of the word *chantier* (construction site). Displaying at once the signs of editorial interference and of the creative process, it exposes the process of its own construction as well as that of Proust's text. By its own definition, then, it resembles the work of *bricolage* or mosaic which, in organicist terms, substitutes an artificial juxtaposition of fragments for inspiration—the genial necessity linking every part of the organic work. Authenticity or artificiality, organic continuity or deliberate *montage:* in their respective methods and visions, these two editions illustrate the alternative that runs through Proust's formulations of the writing process (the Romantic ideal of the inner book on the one hand, reconstruction and perpetual revision on the other).

What it might mean to incorporate the abbreviated version of *Albertine disparue* into an actual through-reading of the *Recherche* is suggested by Le Livre de Poche Classique's reedition of the posthumous volumes as *Sodome et Gomorrhe III, La Fugitive* and *Le Temps retrouvé.* The publication of *Sodome et Gomorrhe III* (edited and introduced by Mauriac Dyer), a single volume composed of *La Prisonnière* and *Albertine disparue,* is presented as the realization of Proust's desire to publish the two Albertine novels together—parts one and two of *Sodome et Gomorrhe III,* as originally advertised by the Nouvelle Revue Française. *Albertine disparue* is followed in a separate volume by *La Fugitive: Cahiers d'Albertine disparue,* the longer, canonical version of the same text.

The result of such an arrangement for the reader—backtracking, overlapping episodes, and nonchronological sequencing—has prompted Milly to compare these volumes to a labyrinth.[16] In fact, the most interesting feature of this recursive reading process is that it uncannily doubles the most dramatic action of the episode, Albertine's death. To return to *La Fugitive* after finishing *Albertine disparue* is to read Albertine's death in both of its versions, the newer version followed by the old: Albertine dies once "on the banks of the Vivonne," confirming the narrator's suspicions with respect to her secret life on the side of Gomorrah, and a second time without resolving any of the ambiguity inherent in the narrative. The work of mourning itself appears twice, once in its foreshortened form and then again in the interminable agony of uncertainty. The story of Albertine, in other words, comes to resemble what Séailles described as the antithesis of organic form. "Il y a des drames qui commencent et finissent deux ou trois fois. Ce n'est pas l'œuvre vivante du génie, ensemble organique de détails subordonnés" (There are dramas that begin and end two or three times. This is not the living work of genius, an organic ensemble of subordinated details) (*Le Génie dans l'art*, 211).

Narrative of Suspicion

Alberto Beretta Anguissola has compared the "sublime pages" Proust eliminated from *Albertine disparue* to literary summits in Dante, Racine, and Dostoyevski. "C'est comme si . . . Racine avait 'biffé' la déclaration de Phèdre à Hippolyte" (It's as though . . . Racine had "crossed out" Phèdre's declaration [of incestuous love] to Hippolyte) ("Le Doute philologique," 72). The comparison summarily underscores the fact that any attempt now to take account of Proust's final revisions must involve the reconstruction of a damaged literary coherence. Such reconstruction has taken various forms in the new editions, but in no case have the "sublime" pages, essential to making sense of the end of the *Recherche*, simply been eliminated. They have been integrated, rather, into new totalities—the totalizing "integral" edition that displays simultaneously all the different stages of composition, the unconventional sequence of posthumous volumes offered by Le Livre de

Poche Classique.

As embodiments of reading strategies, these re-created totalities are subject to criteria for coherence that have little changed since Henri Ghéon charged (just after the appearance of *Du côté de chez Swann*) that Proust refused his readers the satisfactions of the organic whole. "Cette satisfaction organique que nous procure une œuvre dont nous embrassons d'un regard tous les membres, la forme, il nous la refuse obstinément" (That organic satisfaction offered by a work of art whose limbs and form we take in at a single glance, he obstinately refuses to give it to us) (see Chapter 3). When Jean Milly, introducing his edition of *Albertine disparue*, qualifies the Grasset edition as "peu satisfaisant pour les lecteurs" (not very satisfying for readers), he seems to echo Ghéon's complaint about *Swann*. But dissatisfaction has long inhabited the narrative of Albertine and has only taken on a new aspect with the reedition of the posthumous volumes. A certain narrative doubling has been discernible in the story of Albertine from its beginnings—a duality that now plays out logically in the irreducible differences between *La Fugitive* and *Albertine disparue* (most strikingly in the back-to-back pairing of the two versions in *Sodome et Gomorrhe III*).

When Feuillerat turned to examine closely one of those enormous "excrescences" that had transformed *À la recherche du temps perdu*—the "roman d'Albertine"—he discovered that it was composed of two substantially different narratives.[17] The story in its first form, which he reconstructed from internal evidence, was "singularly satisfying": "Elle *forme un tout* et correspond bien au titre ["Les Intermittences du cœur"] par la peinture qu'elle offre du jeu intermittent des sentiments de désir et de satiété qui partageaient le cœur—ou plutôt les sens—du narrateur" (it *forms a whole* and corresponds well to its title ["The Intermittencies of the Heart"] through the portrait it offers of the intermittent feelings of desire and satiety which share the narrator's heart—or rather his senses) (*Comment Marcel Proust*, 203, italics mine). Feuillerat identified an intermediate stage of revision by means of Proust's 1915 dedication of *Du côté de chez Swann* to Madame Scheikévitch, which consists in a lengthy summary of the rest of the novel and features Albertine prominently (*Corr.*, 14:281–

85; *SL*, 3:325–29). Proust's additions, he concluded, created an overwhelming thematics of doubt, suspicion, jealousy and torment—features that now characterize the story of Albertine as we know it (with the fascinating exception of Grasset's *Albertine disparue*). These "corrosive" additions, he claimed, gradually ate away at the coherence of the satisfying whole originally offered by the story of Albertine.

At the heart of Feuillerat's analysis is the very question raised by the rediscovery of Proust's final text: how does revision create or destroy meaning, that is, reinforce or obliterate the coherence of existing narrative patterns? Whereas the Grasset editors' insistence on the unifying role of *Albertine disparue* suggests a willingness to see a powerfully coherent design at work even in Proust's incomplete revisions, for Feuillerat the addition subtracts. The introduction of excessive ambiguity and doubt into the story of Albertine marks the start of a breakdown in narrative coherence and especially a change in *proportion* that will affect the structure of the entire cycle of novels. Indeed, he represents the new narrative of suspicion as the transformation of a nonessential, literally marginal feature (the *soupçon*, or fleeting doubt, the brief addition written onto the manuscript) into the narrative's central feature, its essence. "C'est à peine si l'on peut trouver [dans le résumé de 1915] quelques traces de jalousie, germe de ce qui a fini par devenir l'essentiel" (One finds [in the 1915 summary] only the barest traces of jealousy, a tiny seed of what would become the essential) (210). If the latecomer Albertine has become, as Proust affirmed to Gallimard in 1917, "un principe d'action et le vrai centre de l'ouvrage" (a dramatic principle and the true center of the novel) (Proust and Gallimard, *Correspondance*, 84), Feuillerat's analysis points to a similar displacement at the core of the episode itself. What he describes on a formal level as textual swelling (*boursouflure, gonflement*) corresponds thematically to the growth of jealousy, suspicion, and doubt, the progressive encroachment of an irrational fear.

The claim that Proust's deathbed revisions to *Albertine disparue* effect narrative closure, examined in the light of the peculiar pattern of growth sketched out by Feuillerat, imposes upon us an interesting question. What is it, precisely, that is being closed?

Feuillerat cites Proust's 1915 inscription to Madame Scheikévitch, which designates Albertine as "[le personnage] qui joue le plus grand rôle et amène la péripétie" (the character who plays the most important role and brings the story to a head) and outlines the principal action of the episode: the narrator's jealousy awakened by Albertine's revelation of her friendship with Mademoiselle Vinteuil, followed by their life in common in his Paris apartment, where he keeps her more or less sequestered; Albertine's brusque departure and accidental death, the staggered and repetitive process of mourning, finally the intermittent signs of an approaching indifference. But in its final form, he affirms, the *histoire d'amour* (love story) has turned into an *histoire d'amour angoissé,* suspicion has turned into a terrifying obsession, and love itself has become an *idée fixe.* "Ce qui domine maintenant c'est une histoire d'amour angoissé se détruisant par sa propre inquiétude, obsession plus que passion, car cet amour a tourné à l'idée fixe et finit par perdre, à force de subtilité, toute chaleur et même toute réalité" (What dominates now is an anxious love story which destroys itself through its own anxiety, more an obsession than a passion, for it has turned into an *idée fixe* and ends up losing, through its sophistication, all of its previous warmth and reality) (*Comment Marcel Proust,* 211). The terms in which Feuillerat describes these permutations inevitably suggest a conflation of the story itself with its literary form: where the form has gone awry, has exceeded the parameters of literary normality and is swollen with monstrous outgrowths, the love story has itself become obsessive, unreasonable, and finally morbid.

Significantly, it is a growing focus on Albertine's real or imagined lesbianism that marks this departure from literary and amorous norms, setting apart the two forms of the narrative. For Feuillerat, the most striking result of Proust's additions is precisely that the narrator's obsession with the specter of Gomorrah prevents narrative closure after the death of Albertine:[18]

> Cette crainte de découvrir qu'Albertine est une invertie a pris de telles proportions qu'elle forme dans l'histoire actuelle une affolante obsession, affolante pour le narrateur dont elle obscurcit la raison et affolante pour celle qui en est, sans répit, la victime. Le narrateur est pris par le désir de savoir si Albertine s'adonne

vraiment au vice qu'il la soupçonne d'avoir. . . . Et ce besoin de connaître la vérité persiste, s'exaspère même, après la mort d'Albertine; il se satisfait alors par des enquêtes qui n'ont d'autre résultat que de faire naître des doutes en sens contraire, laissant l'esprit du narrateur dans un désarroi complet (210).

The fear of discovering that Albertine is a lesbian has taken on such proportions that it creates, in the current version of the story, a terrifying obsession, terrifying for the narrator whose reason it obscures and terrifying for its unrelenting object. The narrator is possessed by the desire to know whether Albertine really gives herself over to the vice of which he suspects her. . . . And this need to know the truth persists, is even exacerbated, after Albertine's death; he then pursues investigations which have no other result than to give birth to doubts in the other direction, leaving the mind of the narrator in complete disarray.

What destroys the ostensible coherence of the primary text, growing out of proportion to the rest of the story, is the insatiable desire to know. The anxious additions are conceived of here as narrative excesses, supplemental parts which, according to the organic model, undermine the unity of the whole. Still within the organicist perspective, but especially in its vitalistic, developmental sense, the additions are an afterthought: they spring from one of the contingent elements of the narrative, the "seed" of suspicion contained within the earlier versions but occupying a proportionate space. Feuillerat's analysis of the Albertine episode in its two forms thus reiterates, at the level of the narrative itself, his organicist thesis that the 1913 version of the novel was destroyed by excess. He locates the origin of that excess in a disjunctive creative process, in the temporal fragmentation of a supposedly rational, coherent authorial intention. That split in intention would correspond to two narratives, one placed under the sign of proportion and reason, the other under that of excess and even dementia.

Laurent Jenny has pointed out that the revisions of Flaubert, whose stylistic obsessiveness can be seen as one of the models for Proust's tendency toward perpetual revision, typically moved in the direction of narrative ambiguity and uncertainty. Critical scrutiny of Flaubert's extensive pretextual archive has revealed, writes Jenny, a "strategy of meaning that resembles that of genetic criticism" ("Genetic Criticism," 18)—in other words, that moves away from the closure of the finished form. Is such a strategy of meaning at work in Proust's progressive revisions to the episode of Albertine? In a study devoted exclusively to Proust's additions, Alison Winton gathers under the rubric "Lies and Uncertainty" a large number of revisions tending toward ambiguity. Uncertainty, doubt, instances of lying, and considerations on lying: such additions constitute, she argues, one of the most remarkable expansions in Proust's post-1914 drafts and are the sign of a "powerful new intention" at work (*Proust's Additions*, 1:264). Her findings corroborate Feuillerat's impression that the focus on jealousy and lying in the Albertine affair was a new construct grafted onto the old. The widespread diffusion of lies and lying that Winton finds in Proust's post-1914 additions is most perceptible, of course, in the narrator's *tête-à-tête* with Albertine. But if many of these additions appear to have the function of attributing lies to Albertine, they are offset by others that absolve her of guilt; the real function of the additions, then, is to generate uncertainty. This curious pattern of revision sketches out the very movement of *La Prisonnière* and *Albertine disparue* (*La Fugitive*): a retreat into the internal space of the narrator's endlessly iterable suspicions, where no external event interferes with the vertiginous process by which his hypotheses regarding Albertine displace one another.

But we are left with a paradoxical problem of closure. The ambiguity characteristic of these two volumes, which finds its most intense expression in the narrator's fruitless investigations following the death of Albertine, appears to have been created largely by Proust's revisions. And as we turn to Grasset's *Albertine disparue*, much of that ambiguity disappears in the stroke of a pen with Proust's final, drastic deletions. Exactly as though Proust, right before his death, were revising his own revisions— putting an end to whatever propelled their endless generation of new text. The question is, what kind of an end?

"Cross Out Everything"

The critic Jean de Pierrefeu remarked dryly but perspicaciously in a December 12, 1919, review of *À l'Ombre des jeunes filles en fleurs* for the *Journal des Débats* that "la fatigue ou la mort seules peuvent arrêter [l'auteur] dans la tâche qu'il a entreprise de rechercher le temps perdu par lui" (fatigue or death alone could stop [the author] in his task of searching for time lost—by him). Proust's multiple references to this remark in his correspondence of 1919–20 suggest that the truth of the comment was not lost on him. His response betrays a central preoccupation with questions of textual closure and coherence in relation to (his own) death—a preoccupation dramatically reflected both in the tale of Albertine and in the editorial dilemma posed by Proust's last revisions to *Albertine disparue.* In Chapter 2, I traced an alternative between two distinct kinds of closure that emerge from Proust's correspondence with his publishers: the artificial endings imposed through the editorial process and those motivated by the specific internal logic of a narrative. Proust's long resistance to ending *Du côté de chez Swann* before the seven-hundredth page, and his reluctant concession to his publisher's demands in the form of a "premature ending," provide a striking illustration of this alternative. The distinction between necessary and arbitrary endpoints finally takes the form of an aporia toward the end of his life. Time itself, whatever time is left to him after each declared completion, becomes synonymous with the possibility of further revision, so that the arbitrary endpoints of the fixed published form and of death, imposed from without, inevitably provide closure to a writing process that lacks the particular necessity of an ending.

It is in the Albertine episode that the impossibility of autonomous closure takes an allegorical form. *La Fugitive*—the title by which I will now refer to the longer version of the volume—presents the narrator at an impasse before a proliferation of possible endings, different versions of the story Albertine refuses to tell completely or consistently and which he seeks to reconstruct even long after her death. The question of how to put a stop to the proliferation, resolve the narrative's ambiguities in favor of a particular version, is rigorously parallel to the question now faced by editors of this volume, that is, whether to grant a definitive, transforming status to Proust's final revisions and thus to "revise," not merely retrospectively but *retroactively,* the meaning of Albertine's story.

Critics have often remarked that the Albertine volumes are most explicitly preoccupied with jealousy as an epistemological drive. Indeed, *La Fugitive* seems to exemplify the search for truth that Proust at least nominally identified as his larger project (*Corr.*, 13:99). Leo Bersani has rightly observed that love is portrayed in these volumes as "a compulsive intellectual investigation" (*Marcel Proust*, 61); in his *Freud, Proust and Lacan*, Malcolm Bowie devotes a separate chapter to the problem of jealousy as knowledge ("Proust, Jealousy, Knowledge"), concluding that jealousy is "the quest for knowledge in a terrifying pure form: a quest for knowledge untrammelled and unsupported by things actually known" (58). Peter Brooks calls sexual jealousy in the *Recherche* "the very principle of epistemology," specifying that in *La Fugitive* we encounter the most extreme epistemological anguish of the entire novel: "the mad desire to know another person's past, to fill in the gaps created by absences and lies, the need constantly to revise the narrative of one's life through discoveries about another's biography" (*Body Work*, 118, 121). It is precisely because the desire to know takes the form of a "need to revise" that the narrative of obsessive investigation comes to allegorize its own writing, a writing heavily marked by revision: additions and deletions whose own coherence, with that of the text they modify and with one another, has been in question since Feuillerat. The need for revision is represented within the narrative as the interpretive effort to derive coherence from a story delivered in fragments, fragments elicited first from Albertine herself and later, in the canonical *Fugitive*, from diverse informants whose contradictory and incomplete accounts of her life displace one another temporarily but without adding up or forming an intelligible whole. This process of revision inscribed in the narrative nearly always moves, like Proust's additions, in the direction of ambiguity and uncertainty.

In *Postmodern Proust*, Margaret Gray argues that the ultimate failure of these epistemological efforts is paradigmatic of a pattern of failed mastery throughout the *Recherche*, a "failure to understand and master the world through knowledge" (64). Gray puts into question a critical tradition that echoes the narrator's claims to mastery, control, and objectivity. The characteristic undecidability of *La Fugitive*—its refusal to provide resolution to the dichotomies pervading the narrator's epistemological discourse (Albertine is either truthful or a liar, faithful or treacherous, heterosexual or lesbian)—is not effaced, she argues, by the apparent closure of *Albertine disparue*. "No matter what the edition of *Albertine disparue*, Albertine has always already, in *La Prisonnière*, overturned all attempts to derive a coherent narrative that would explain her mysterious sexual past and inclinations, confining her within a history" (97). Gray then insists on the strictly *interpretive* nature of the apparent certainty that dispenses with the narrator's inquisition in the form of Proust's final addition. If the latter appears to resolve the ambiguity of Albertine, allowing the narrative to come to an end, it does so only through an act of interpretation on the part of the narrator, who willingly sees definitive evidence of Albertine's perfidiousness (and her homosexuality) in the revised announcement of her death.[19] This emphasis on the subjective character of the narrative closure achieved by the addition points, in fact, to a perfect coincidence of Proust's final revisional gesture with that of his narrator: closure is represented in *Albertine disparue* as the willful imposition of choice in the face of multiple possibilities, as contingent and artificial rather than as a necessary development of the narrative itself.

The tale of proliferating suspicion, read as an allegory of a writing process seeking closure, can now be said to contain a representation of closure that inscribes the text with a model for stopping the excesses of discourse, ending the process of revision. That model is best seized in Proust's second addition relative to Albertine's death in *Albertine disparue* (quoted in part above), where the narrator attributes a precise and devastating meaning to the site of Albertine's fatal accident:

> Ces mots: "au bord de la Vivonne," ajoutaient quelque chose de plus atroce à mon désespoir. Car cette coïncidence qu'elle m'eût dit dans le petit tram qu'elle était amie de Mademoiselle Vinteuil, et que l'endroit où elle était depuis qu'elle m'avait quitté et où elle avait trouvé la mort fût le voisinage de Montjouvain, cette coïncidence ne pouvait être fortuite, un éclair jaillissait entre ce Montjouvain raconté dans le chemin de fer et cette Vivonne involontairement avouée dans le télégramme de Madame Bontemps. Et c'était donc le soir où j'étais allé chez les Verdurin, le

soir où je lui avais dit vouloir la quitter, qu'elle m'avait menti! (*Albertine disparue* [Grasset], 111–12).

Those words: "on the banks of the Vivonne," added an atrocious note to my despair. For the coincidence of these two things—Albertine having told me in the tram that she was a friend of Mademoiselle Vinteuil, and the fact that she met with her death in the vicinity of Montjouvain—this coincidence could hardly be fortuitous; a flash went off between this Montjouvain mentioned in the train and this Vivonne involuntarily confessed in Madame Bontemps's telegram. And so it was the evening when I went to the Verdurins', the evening when I told her I wanted to leave her, that she had lied to me!

The conflicting hypotheses that have subtended much of the narrator's discourse have taken a specific form in the alternative evoked above. Albertine, the narrator reasons, was lying on one of two occasions, either when she made the claim to know Mademoiselle Vinteuil or when she subsequently overturned the same claim. The posthumous "confession"—"cette Vivonne involontairement avouée" (this involuntarily confessed Vivonne)—brings about a spontaneous reinterpretation of the ambiguous past in the form of a certainty. The resolution of this alternative is definitive, for it forecloses the postmortem investigation that originally followed the announcement of Albertine's death. The closure represented in this passage is of the kind Proust identified as editorial: a decision to end the text by imposing on it, a posteriori—that is, onto a completed text—new definition in the form of abridgment of material. Unlike many of Proust's interpolations, the additions to *Albertine disparue* are not accompanied by the corresponding preparations whose purpose was to create the illusion that the new elements were integral, logical developments of the existing narrative; instead, they confirm a possible reading of the text into which they are interpolated, representing the very act of interpretation they put into effect. The narrative coherence of *Albertine disparue* thus revised is entirely an effect of this "editorial" choice. For not only does the passage above mark a moment of interpretation, it suggests in its conviction that we do the same, that we read the Albertine episode, retrospectively, as though it now told a different story.

Feuillerat's sense that something had gotten out of hand, so to speak, in *La Prisonnière* and *La Fugitive* has been echoed by critics who see in the short version of *Albertine disparue* a corrective to the putative excesses of *La Fugitive*. While the Pléiade editors suggest that Proust's cuts put an end to a kind of narrative rut, "l'interminable travail du deuil et de la jalousie dans lequel s'engluait l'action" (the interminable work of mourning and jealousy in which the action was getting bogged down) (*RTP*, 4:1030), Mauriac Dyer has asserted that the cuts have a corrective function both narratively and structurally ("Cycle," 69). Christie McDonald has similarly called Proust's elimination of material a "means to clarity," specifying that Proust made *Albertine disparue* "more dramatic *and coherent* by putting a stop to both the jealousy and the mourning" (*The Proustian Fabric*, 150, italics mine). McDonald explicitly links Proust's revisions to the excesses of epistemology: "The cuts may have made manageable an excessive text dealing with the excessive compulsion to knowledge: of Albertine" (152). From this point of view, "outgrowth" is not only textual excess with respect to a previous narrative structure; it is also the madness connected with jealousy, homosexuality, the compulsion to know.[20]

Proust's last editorial gesture, his order to "cross out everything"—the phrase by which he instructed his housekeeper and confidante Céleste Albaret to make the deletions (*Corr.*, 21:515)—constitutes an interpretive choice in favor of one of the narrative's possibilities, undoing its very motor. If we bear in mind that Proust transformed the story of Albertine into a narrative of suspicion (through his additions) and ultimately sacrificed the apogee of that movement in *Albertine disparue*, then his final gesture of elimination, which stops proliferation *within the narrative*, coincides with an effort to stop the process of revision itself. As such, it appears to be the only moment of self-imposed arrest in a process of inexorable textual expansion that intensified in the last few years of Proust's life—a moment in which Proust willingly took on the "containing" role editing had always played for him, freely choosing to set new limits for the volume rather than conceding to them gradually under editorial pressure. (A January 1922 letter to Gallimard speaks eloquently on this late expansion.

Proust assured Gallimard, who had begun to worry about the growing number of volumes, that it was not too late for him to look for another publisher if *À la recherche du temps perdu* was becoming too "vast" for the Nouvelle Revue Française [*Corr.*, 21:40].) What had gotten out of hand, in other words, was writing—and rewriting. Proust's final revisions curtail simultaneously the thematics of uncontrolled suspicion, the extended process of mourning, and (extradiegetically) the compulsive rewriting through which both had come to dominate *La Fugitive.* It is tempting to suggest that the writing of jealousy and mourning, so clearly connected to a real-life source of grief, had served its purpose and was now to be reabsorbed in a larger fictional structure whose lines remain, at the present writing, unknown to us.

Rereading the Recherche

Proust consistently linked the activity of correcting his proofs to his own death, evoking its imminent threat whenever he was presented with a new set of proofs to correct or even tying the progression of his illness to the labor of revision. A 1918 letter to Lucien Daudet is typical. "Je voudrais bien pouvoir corriger les épreuves de mon livre, mais pense qu'il y a cinq volumes. Comment vivre jusque-là, sans compter le reste. Il faut un an pour corriger les épreuves d'un volume" (I'd love to be able to correct the proofs of my book, but imagine that there are five volumes. How to stay alive until then, without counting the rest. It takes a year to correct the proofs of one volume) (*Corr.*, 17:170). This reiterated link can be understood as a paradigm of the particular relationship of the writing process to reading, a reading always menaced, like writing, with incompletion. For behind these references a motif appears, a desire Proust repeatedly articulated as a condition for finishing the *Recherche:* to reread the entire novel from end to end, on the proofs themselves, before finishing his corrections. The complete linear reading that Proust had so emphatically recommended to the first readers of *Swann* as a requisite to comprehension of the first volume—"bien peu de chose dans son ensemble" (very little indeed within the larger whole) (*Corr.*, 12:255)—had become a necessary condition for writing. "Car pour un livre si long, où ont pu se glisser des répétitions, des double-emplois, il est utile que je relise d'un bout à l'autre l'ouvrage" (For a book so long, into which repetitions and redundancies might have slipped, it would be useful for me to reread the work from end to end) (Proust and Gallimard, *Correspondance,* 72). The incoherencies that have become familiar to readers of Proust since his death—contradictions, repetitions, inexplicable resuscitations— were understood by Proust as an inscription of the passage of time, in the form of forgetting, into the text. But if these lapses were the natural result of an extended writing time, the corollary process of rereading he proposed as a remedy was itself too long for Proust to complete. He would die, in effect, without having reread, "from end to end," *À la recherche du temps perdu.* This desire for a linear reading, and its impossibility, illuminate the specifically nonlinear, *nontextual,* nature of the metaphors Proust chose to represent the coherence of his work (see Chapter 2): the totalizing unity of the *tableau,* tapestry or vase, referring back to a coherence of conception, conjures away the troubling resemblance of the text, in its linearity, to a life lived from one end to the other and always subject to interruption.

The rereading that would have permitted Proust to uncover his own incoherencies has been effected in his stead by several generations of editors and readers, as attention has come to be focused on cracks in the vase, loose threads running through the tapestry. Starting with the first posthumous editing of the 1920s, editions of the *Recherche* have followed a perceptible trajectory, moving from the artful disguise of incoherence to its unveiling. This tendency toward exposing the gaps and faults of the text such as Proust left it is tantamount to a collective reading, the one Proust did not have time to do. It culminates in the multiple editions that have become available since the 1980s, some of which frankly present themselves as deconstructions of a long-established and perpetuated illusion of coherence. That illusion, however, has come undone gradually with each successive wave of editions, as editors have chosen to reveal various aspects of the text's incompletion, and as readers have themselves noted traces of incompletion that even the Nouvelle Revue Française's practice of textual air-brushing could not disguise. When *Albertine disparue* appeared in book-

stores in 1925, reviewers were overwhelmingly struck by its lack
of polish, its draft-like character.[21] And in 1936, with only the original edition to consult, Philip Kolb published an essay on the
"inadvertent repetitions" he found throughout the *Recherche*—
duplications of the kind Proust had hoped to eliminate before publication. Kolb ended his inquiry with a hope to contribute to the
establishment of a critical text by "exposing the mechanics of the
creative process" (262). When a critical edition materialized some
twenty years later in the form of a Pléiade volume (1954), its editors, Pierre Clarac and André Ferré, effectively conserved the more
conspicuous inconsistencies of the posthumous volumes (notably
the deaths and subsequent reappearances of Bergotte, Cottard, and
Madame de Villeparisis)—an editorial decision that marked a significant departure from the strategy of the Nouvelle Revue
Française editors.[22] The discovery and publication of Proust's last
corrected text, compromising the traditional readability of the
posthumous volumes, can be seen as the latest stage in a continuous process of unveiling incoherence. Indeed, we seem to have
entered, to borrow Nathalie Sarraute's phrase, an "era of suspicion" with regard to the completion and coherence of the Proustian text in its canonical form.

But has Grasset taken his revenge? The authority of the Gallimard editions, and notably that of the Pléiade (Gallimard's Collection Blanche, Collection Folio, and Collection Quarto
reproduce the Pléiade text), has yet to be unseated.[23] The legacy of
the original Nouvelle Revue Française edition is still clearly
apparent in the introduction to the most recent Pléaide, where we
read that although *La Prisonnière*, *Albertine disparue*, and *Le
Temps retrouvé* bear numerous errors and inconsistencies, *À la
recherche du temps perdu* "n'est nullement une œuvre incom-
plète" (is in no way an incomplete work) (*RTP*, 1:ciii). The ambiguity of this statement has been key to the ethos of the canonical
Recherche ever since the 1920s: traces of incompletion are
acknowledged and exposed only on the condition of maintaining
the coherence and solidity of the whole.

At the heart of this practice is an understanding of complete-
ness that embraces Proust's own strategies for defining coherence
as the articulation between beginning and end. (Surely it is no

coincidence that the director of the 1987–89 Pléiade edition, Jean-Yves Tadié, stands behind the ideology of preliminary poetic closure, maintaining that Proust's coordination of the first and last chapters created a circular structure that "was not compromised by any external event, neither the meeting with Agostinelli, nor the First World War" [*Marcel Proust*, 761].) Integrated into the *Recherche*, Grasset's *Albertine disparue* would demolish precisely the framework that Proust repeatedly invoked as both the proof and the symbol of his "construction." This is no doubt why it remains in the margins—an extraordinarily important document but not an integral part of *À la recherche du temps perdu*. Like Grasset's 1913 edition of *Du côté de chez Swann*, it commemorates a significant moment in a living process but has itself become a kind of museum piece.

Epilogue

Proust's letters to Gallimard contain frequent complaints about delays in the publication of his books, despite the fact that his perpetual revisions were themselves the cause of more than a few delays. In November 1918, he reminded Gallimard of his desire to oversee the entire publication of *À la recherche du temps perdu*—in other words, he added, to stay alive until the process was finished. He went on to detail a series of printer's delays that were making it, he thought, unlikely that he would. "Maintenant je vois qu'il ne faudra pas un an pour les quatre volumes comme vous m'aviez dit, mais huit ans! Or (comme les trois derniers volumes . . . paraîtront ensemble), quand ils paraîtront (c'est-à-dire, de ce train-là, vers 1925, au plus tôt), à supposer que l'auteur soit toujours en vie pour corriger ses épreuves, les lecteurs auront depuis longtemps oublié l'existence de Swann, et le tout sera raté" (Now I see that the four volumes will take not a year, as you'd said, but eight years! But [since the last three volumes . . . will appear together], when they appear [that is, at this rate, around 1925 at the earliest], assuming that the author is still alive to correct his proofs, my readers will have long forgotten the existence of Swann and the whole thing will fall flat) (*Corr.*, 17:442). Proust was not far off in his facetious estimate of 1925, since his final volume appeared in 1927. Quite apart from the time of writing, the time of publication presented its own perils for the reading process—technical matters over which he had no control, such as the printer's insistence on finishing one volume before setting the next into proofs. Each of these delays contributed to what Proust articulated as a possible disaster for his novel: the reader's failure to remember the beginning by the time the end came into print.

Perhaps he would not have been surprised, then, to learn that the most recent English translation of the *Recherche*—Penguin's six-volume, seven-part *In Search of Lost Time* (published in Britain in 2002)—will appear in the United States over a period of some sixteen years, due to American copyright law. *Swann's Way* appeared in 2003, followed by three more volumes in 2004; but Viking Press will have to wait until at least 2019 to publish the end of the novel.[1] Of course, American readers who began with *Swann's Way* in 2003 might opt to order the last two British volumes over the Internet rather than risk forgetting Swann by 2020 when *Finding Time Again* hits the bookstores. And yet this very important translation, the first complete English translation of the *Recherche* since the 1920s, was conceived in the view of a simultaneous publication: Penguin's choice to have seven different translators working at once clearly shows that time was of the essence (Proust's original translator, C. K. Scott Moncrieff, died in 1930 before completing the last volume). Subject to the arbitrariness of public domain law, the Viking edition beautifully confirms the logic of Proust's reiterated efforts to safeguard the unity of his work against fragmentation and delay—that is, external, nonliterary delay. It also confirms, by its very existence, the vitality of his worldwide readership at the start of the twenty-first century, a readership willing to perform the work of reassembling the whole on their own time and their own terms—which is exactly what Proust asked of the reader (*Corr.*, 12:222).

Spread out in time and now expanded in volume, *À la recherche du temps perdu* grew, in the Bibliothèque de la Pléiade, from 3,500 to over 7,000 pages between 1954 and 1989. This expansion, which was due to the inclusion of drafts and variants now in the public domain, has prompted some critics to decry the annihilation of the text as a distinct, autonomous object, its dissolution in a sea of possible alternative versions.[2] On the contrary, the canonical Pléiade edition, with its exhaustive pretextual archive, invites genetic criticism within a teleological perspective. Sketches and variants are included in the volume, but formally excluded from the text itself, in the view of shoring up the literary work as monument, not melting it down. They are presented as fragments of a single-minded creative enterprise, as stages along the path toward the realization of the One Book (*Jean Santeuil* and *Contre Sainte-Beuve* are recuperated as failed attempts en route). Far from diminishing the status of the *Recherche* as an independent book, Gallimard has become the guardian of Proust's topos of simultaneous poetic closure, while maintaining the work's completion in a more concrete sense as well. For Jean-Yves Tadié, this has meant a categorical dismissal of Proust's last revised text as an "experimental version" carried out by a "semi-comatose" creator in his final days. "Just as some people on their deathbed disinherit their family so as to leave everything to their nurse, Proust removed some of the finest passages from Albertine in order to bestow them on a hypothetical 'Sodome IV or V'" (*Marcel Proust*, 773). Because Proust did not have time to produce the imagined volume that would have absorbed the 250 pages he omitted, Tadié concludes, "the spirit should prevail over the letter" in the matter of *Albertine disparue* (774).

The violence of Tadié's portrayal of Proust on his deathbed—the half-unconscious, irresponsible creator capable of only reckless actions—is a telling index of the feverish pitch to which the opposition of spirit and letter has risen with respect to Proust's completion of the *Recherche*. As I have tried to show in *Proust's Deadline*, the completion upon which Proust insisted from the start was a crucial element in a symbolic structure that included the anticipation of future fragmentation and rupture. Because of Proust's extraordinary awareness that he was writing against a deadline, his writing experience can be considered a (perhaps unparalleled) experiment with time: an experiment where the effort to compress the time of writing into the closed form of the book was inevitably disrupted by the raw, persistent energy of lived temporality.

When Proust wrote to René Blum in 1913 that his nearly finished novel was in need of a "tomb"—a published form—before his own was filled, he alluded to the vitalistic notion that identifies the fixing of text in print with the death of the living, changing work (*Corr.*, 12:80). Displayed upon pages and enclosed within volumes, materialized as *À la recherche du temps perdu*, the time of writing thus appears to be eclipsed by the literal closure of the book. But Albertine has never stopped disrupting finished meaning—her return to the center of debate long after Proust's death is an echo of her unsettling invention, a resurgence of uncertainty at the heart of the fixed form.

NOTES

Introduction

1. Quoted by Painter, *Marcel Proust,* 2:293.

2. Roger Shattuck, for example, long argued that the *Recherche* was excessively long and should be pared down to its allegedly universal elements. His suggestions for what should be omitted—most of *Sodome et Gomorrhe,* much of *La Prisonnière,* and all of *Albertine disparue*—betrayed a nostalgia for the 1913 version of Proust's novel, which excluded the *Sodome et Gomorrhe* cycle (*Proust's Way,* 25). In *Le Hors-sujet,* Bayard has a chapter on the various "reductionist schools" of Proust criticism ("Longueurs," 11–16).

3. [Günther] Müller's classic distinction between *Erzählzeit* (the time of narration) and *erzählte Zeit* (narrated time) is of some pertinence here, although neither Müller nor [Gérard] Genette after him theorizes the time of reading itself (see Müller, "Erzählzeit und erzählte Zeit"). In *Figures III,* Genette defines *Erzählzeit* as a temporality belonging to the text alone—a *faux temps* (false time), a temporality borrowed from the reading process (77–78). Ricœur, in *Temps et récit II,* assimilates Müller's *Erzählzeit* to the time of reading (113–20), but for Ricœur the time of reading is simply the corollary of the time of narration. I am interested here in an aspect of *Erzählzeit* that has been insufficiently defined: the time of reading in its relationship to the time of production (writing and publishing).

4. This much-commented passage from *Le Temps retrouvé* plays an indispensable hermeneutical role for the entire cycle of novels, since it forms a part of the hero-narrator's decision to embrace his vocation as a writer. "On peut faire se succéder indéfiniment dans une description les objets qui figuraient dans le lieu décrit, la vérité ne commencera qu'au moment où l'écrivain prendra deux objets différents, posera leur rapport, analogue dans le monde de l'art à celui qu'est le rapport unique de la loi causale dans le monde de la science, et les enfermera dans les anneaux nécessaires d'un beau style. Même, ainsi que la vie, quand en rapprochant une qualité commune à deux sensations, il dégagera leur essence commune en les réunissant l'une et l'autre pour les soustraire aux contingences du temps, dans une métaphore" ([The writer] can describe a scene by describing one after another the innumerable objects which at a given moment were present at a particular place, but truth will be attained by him only when he takes two different objects, states the connexion

119

between them—a connexion analogous in the world of art to the unique connexion which in the world of science is provided by the law of causality—and encloses them in the necessary links of a well-wrought style; truth—and life too—can be attained by us only when, by comparing a quality common to two sensations, we succeed in extracting their common essence and in reuniting them to each other, liberated from the contingencies of time, within a metaphor) (*RTP*, 4:468; *Remembrance*, 3:924–25).

5. See, for example, Ellison's "Proustian Metaphor and the Question of Readability," in *The Reading of Proust* (1–29), and Gray's "Figuration and Resistance," in *Postmodern Proust* (115–37).

6. For a historical overview of the symbol-allegory opposition, see Krieger, "The 'Imaginary' and Its Enemies."

7. The organic paradigm in literary theory can be traced back to classical antiquity, and especially to Plato's *Phaedrus* (360 BC). Its defining modern expression is typically found in the Romantic aesthetics that descended from German Idealism largely by way of Samuel Taylor Coleridge, who borrowed from and elaborated upon the theses of Schelling and Schlegel. The legacy of Romantic organicism to modern criticism is a fundamental opposition between mechanical and organic unity, notably formulated by Coleridge in his essay "Shakespeare's Judgment Equal to His Genius" (1818). On the temporal aspects of nineteenth-century organic theory, see Krieger's *A Reopening of Closure*, Chapter 2, 31–56.

8. Henry has treated Proust's German Romantic heritage at length in *Théories pour une esthétique*, in part through a demonstration of Séailles's influence. Raimond and Fraisse give an excellent overview of the ties between Séailles's work and the *Recherche* in *Proust en toutes lettres* (51–54). See also Kristeva, "Proust the Philosopher," in *Time and Sense* (251–75).

9. See Pugh's chapter "Beyond the Grasset Volume," in *The Growth of À la recherche du temps perdu*, 2:703–90.

10. Several volumes of the *Recherche* entered the public domain years earlier, notably those that had appeared posthumously. Grasset's *Albertine disparue*, on the other hand, will remain protected by copyright fifty years following the date of its publication. On the complicated laws that govern literary and artistic property in France, see Ippolito, "À la recherche du temps protégé."

11. Mauriac Dyer has specifically linked the reception of this episode as a "traumatic event" to the corporal basis for the organicist metaphor—that is, the text as body. "La résurgence de la dactylographie originale a constitué, semble-t-il, un événement traumatique, une sorte d'attentat à ce qui est conçu comme une entité physique et vivante—*organisme* et *corps*" (The resurgence of the original typescript has constituted, it seems, a traumatic event, a sort of attack upon what is conceived of as a physical and living entity—*organism* and *body*) ("Proust procruste," 131). As Mauriac Dyer points out, *À la recherche du temps perdu* never existed as the organic, unified book-object that such a reception supposes.

Chapter 1: Forthcoming

1. René Blum (1878–1942), the younger brother of statesman Léon Blum, played the important role of intermediary between Proust and publisher Bernard Grasset. He died at Auschwitz during the Second World War.

2. Bernard de Fallois first published the reassembled fragments of Proust's original project under the title *Contre Sainte-Beuve* in 1954; a very different version was then produced by Pierre Clarac in 1971. Accordinging to Philip Kolb, editor of the *Correspondance*, Proust is alluding here to having completed an early version of the opening section, "Combray," and a draft of the novel's conclusion as he then conceived it: a long conversation between the hero and his mother on the literary critic Sainte-Beuve (*Corr.*, 9:165, n. 5).

3. See, for example, Pugh, *The Birth of* À la recherche du temps perdu (84–87), or Tadié, *Proust et le roman* (241–42). Kolb gives a classic description of Proust's putative illumination as a "fateful moment" in the summer of 1909 that marked the transformation of Sainte-Beuve into a novel (*Le Carnet de 1908*, 20). At the other end of the spectrum is Henry, who remarks dryly that if Proust had an "illumination," it was in the classrooms of the Sorbonne—and that it would take him another twenty-five years of writing to give his "revelation" a form (*Proust romancier*, 25).

4. Perhaps most famously in a letter to Jacques Rivière, just a few months after the publication of *Du côté de chez Swann*: "Enfin je trouve un lecteur qui *devine* que mon livre est un ouvrage dogmatique et une construction!" (At last I find a reader who *grasps* that my book is a dogmatic work and a construction!) (*Corr.*, 13:98).

5. The proofs of the second Grasset volume, entitled *Le Côté de Guermantes*, corresponded in large part to *À l'Ombre des jeunes filles en fleurs* and to the beginning of what is now *Le Côté de Guermantes I*. See Alden, *Marcel Proust's Grasset Proofs*, 14–15.

6. On Proust's change in publishers during the war years, see my essay "Mea Culpa." Boillat recounts Proust's change in publishers from Grasset's point of view in *La Librairie Bernard Grasset et les lettres françaises*, 174–202.

7. See Robert, "L'Édition des posthumes d'*À la recherche du temps perdu*." The insert also appeared in the January 1, 1923, issue of *La Nouvelle Revue Française*, "Hommage à Marcel Proust."

8. An October 1909 letter to Anna de Noailles is typical: "J'ai commencé à travailler. Et jusqu'à ce que mon travail soit fini . . . je ne veux pas risquer les moindres fatigues qui, dans mon état devenu si précaire, sont de grands dangers. Mais si je peux continuer et finir cela, si je ne suis pas mort avant . . . " (I have begun to work. And until my work is finished . . . I do not want to risk the slightest fatigue, which in my now precarious condition is highly dangerous. But if I can continue and finish it, if I don't die beforehand . . .) (*Corr.*, 9:196; *SL*, 2:452).

9. Anatole Frances's *L'Orme du mail* and Maurice Barrès's *Les Déracinés* both appeared in 1897.

10. In *La Bibliographie de la France*, Part 3, November 14, 1913. "Après un long silence . . . Marcel Proust, dont les débuts dans les lettres avaient suscité la plus unanime admiration, nous donne sous le titre: *À la Recherche du Temps Perdu* une trilogie dont le premier volume: *Du côté de chez Swann*, est la magistrale introduction" (After a long silence . . . Marcel Proust, whose debut in the world of letters aroused the most unanimous admiration, gives us under the title *À la Recherche du Temps Perdu* a trilogy whose first volume, *Du côté de chez Swann*, serves as its masterful introduction) (3726–27).

11. In *Theory of the Avant-Garde*, Bürger defines the organic work of art as "constructed according to the syntagmatic pattern; individual parts and the whole form a dialectical unity. An adequate reading is described by the hermeneutic circle: the parts can be understood only through the whole, the whole only through the parts. This means that an anticipating comprehension of the whole guides, and is simultaneously corrected by, the comprehension of the parts" (80).

12. This apt expression appears in one of Proust's first letters to publisher Gaston Gallimard (December 1912). Proust tried to persuade Gallimard that a reading of the first seven hundred pages of his manuscript should suffice to form a judgment of the whole—since it was in fact a single book arbitrarily cut into two (*Corr.*, 11:321).

13. Proust defined the notion of "involuntary memory" in his November 1913 interview with *Le Temps*. "Mon œuvre est dominée par la distinction entre la mémoire involontaire et la mémoire volontaire. . . . Pour moi, la mémoire volontaire, qui est surtout une mémoire de l'intelligence et des yeux, ne nous donne du passé que des faces sans vérité; mais qu'une odeur, une saveur retrouvées dans des circonstances toutes différentes, réveille en nous, malgré nous, le passé, nous sentons combien ce passé était différent de ce que nous croyions nous rappeler, et que notre mémoire volontaire peignait . . . avec des couleurs sans vérité" (My work is dominated by the distinction between involuntary and voluntary memory . . . For me, voluntary memory, which is above all a memory of the intelligence and of the eyes, gives us nothing of the past but its inauthentic aspects; but if a smell or a taste, rediscovered in entirely different circumstances, reawakens in us, in spite of us, the past, we sense how much this past differs from everything we thought we remembered about it, everything that our voluntary memory painted . . . with inauthentic colors) (interview with Élie-Joseph Bois, reproduced in Lhomeau and Coelho, *Marcel Proust*, 264–69).

14. See Lhomeau and Coelho, *Marcel Proust* ("Les Feuilletons fantômes du *Figaro*," 39–51). For an excellent discussion of serialization in relation to the distinction between essay and novel, see Fraisse, "Méthode de composition."

15. The verb *rebouter* is used principally in a medical context: it means "to set," as one sets a fracture so that it will heal properly.

16. Proust wrote to Bernard Grasset in February 1913: "J'avais mis provisoirement un titre particulier pour le premier volume. Mais il me semble que le mieux serait de l'appeler *Le Temps perdu Première partie* et l'autre *Le Temps perdu Deuxième partie* puisque en réalité c'est un seul ouvrage" (I had previously given the first volume an individual title. But I think the best thing would be to call it *Le Temps perdu Première partie* and the second one *Le Temps perdu Deuxième partie*, since in reality it's a single book) (*Corr.*, 12:97; *SL*, 3:161). Similarly, in a letter to Georges de Lauris a few months later, Proust mentioned the excerpts that had appeared in *Le Figaro*, adding: "Mais le vrai livre n'est pas là" (But that's not the real book) (*Corr.*, 12:229).

Chapter 2: The Dream of Simultaneous Publication

1. These 712 typed pages comprised about half of what he had written; the other half was not yet in typescript. Lhomeau and Coelho point out that Proust's figure of 712 pages is misleading, since he had numbered many of the pages *bis, ter, quater,* and *quinque* to make room for interpolated pages and passages (*Marcel Proust*, 63).

2. According to Parinet, the *crise de la librairie* began around 1880 and lasted some twenty years. Pointing to the economic recession of the 1880s as a contributing factor, Parinet also suggests that a general disaffection for the reading of fiction had taken hold—and that reading was losing ground against leisure activities such as photography, bicycling, and motorism ("L'Édition littéraire," 158–60).

3. That material continuity finally became a reality in 1999, when Gallimard published *À la recherche du temps perdu* in one 2,408-page volume (Collection Quarto).

4. I discuss Séailles in my Introduction. The expression "philosophy of genius" belongs to Henry, who specifically suggests that Séailles's aesthetic theory was the inspiration for *Jean Santeuil* (*Théories pour une esthétique*, 98–165).

5. While such metaphors seem to refer back to Séailles's use of visual art as the paradigm for all forms of art, the reading process Proust prescribes also points "forward" to structuralism. In his structuralist classic, *Forme et signification*, Rousset compares the volume to a "tableau en mouvement" which is uncovered by successive fragments. "La tâche du lecteur exigeant consiste à renverser cette tendance naturelle du livre, de manière que celui-ci se présente tout entier au regard de l'esprit. Il n'y a de lecture complète que celle qui transforme le livre en un réseau simultané de relations réciproques" (The task of the demanding reader is to reverse this natural tendency of the book, so that the latter presents itself as a whole

to the gaze of the mind. The only complete reading is a reading that transforms the book into a simultaneous network of reciprocal relations) (xiii).

6. Proust will later respond to Paul Souday's charge that certain passages of *Du côté de chez Swann* are gratuitous by affirming the importance of the interval in reading: their function will become clear, he explains, after a certain delay (*Corr.*, 18:464).

7. On this episode, see Hayman, "Rejection," in his *Proust* (346–62), and Carter, "In Search of a Publisher," *Marcel Proust* (507–27).

8. Publication at the author's expense (*à compte d'auteur*) was a common procedure at this time for first-time authors. Parinet remarks that Bernard Grasset Editions, in particular, survived its first seven years largely because it published so many beginning authors *à compte d'auteur* ("L'Édition littéraire," 184). Proust's determination to publish at his own expense was also a question of maintaining control over the conditions of publication, as his letter to Blum clearly indicates.

9. According to Proust's paraphrase of Robert in a March 1913 letter to Jean-Louis Vaudoyer (*Corr.*, 12:117). Robert's letter to Proust has not been conserved.

10. The reader's report by Jacques Normand was first published in *Le Figaro* of December 8, 1966. It is reproduced in Lhomeau and Coelho, *Marcel Proust*, 255–62.

11. "La loi de corrélation organique exige que tous les organes de l'être vivant se répondent et conspirent. Si quelque partie de l'œuvre d'art tout à coup prend un développement inattendu, toutes les autres parties se modifient, pour ne pas composer un être monstrueux" (The law of organic correlation demands that the various organs of a living being respond to one another and conspire. If some part of the work of art takes on an unexpected development, all of the other parts modify themselves accordingly, so as not to create a monstrous being) (Séailles, *Le Génie dans l'art*, 175).

12. For a definitive genetic analysis of Proust's modifications to the Grasset typescript, see Pugh, "The Ending of *Swann* Revisited."

13. Quoted by Séailles: "Il faut qu'un tableau soit peint d'un seul coup de pinceau" (*Le Génie dans l'art*, 213). Félix Ravaisson is best known as the author of *De l'habitude* (1838).

14. As Lhomeau and Coelho remark, "C'est le point de cassure qui l'a emporté sur le point d'orgue; c'est-à dire l'édition proprement dite, sur la littérature" (It was the breaking point that was victorious over the pedal point; that is, editing itself over literature) (*Marcel Proust*, 150).

15. Deferral plays, of course, an essential role in the *Recherche* itself and might even be seen as its subject. The hero-narrator's inability to write—"procrastination," as the Baron de Charlus calls it—serves as a central thread that leads the reader ultimately to the hero-narrator's epiphany in *Le Temps retrouvé:* his long-deferred decision to become a writer.

Chapter 3: Organicism Gone Awry

1. Reproduced by Lhomeau and Coelho, *Marcel Proust*, 283. Compagnon remarks that critics "almost universally reproached the first volumes of the *Recherche,* in particular *Du côté de chez Swann,* for . . . the novel's diversity and 'pulverization,' its absence of organization, form, and choices" (*Proust Between Two Centuries,* 29).

2. See Poulet's alternative to simultaneous perception of the whole, which he calls "memory of the total work": the reader's "final retrospective and elucidating gaze," which turns the discontinuous, juxtaposed episodes into a coherent ensemble whose parts refer to one another and reciprocally illuminate each other (*Proustian Space,* 103–4).

3. According to Bourget's classic definition, "Un style de décadence est celui où l'unité du livre se décompose pour laisser la place à l'indépendance de la page, où la page se décompose pour laisser la place à l'indépendance de la phrase, et la phrase pour laisser la place à l'indépendance du mot" (A decadent style is a style in which the unity of the book decomposes to give way to the independence of the page, where the page decomposes to give way to the independence of the sentence, and the sentence to give way to the independence of the word) (*Essais de psychologie contemporaine,* 25).

4. See Compagnon, *Proust Between Two Centuries,* 31.

5. From Faÿ's recollections of his conversations with Proust, recorded in *Les Précieux:* "Mon livre est une construction, et là réside le travail essentiel pour moi, le travail le plus délicat, du reste. Il faut relier chaque partie à la précédante, annoncer ce qui viendra tout en ménageant la part de l'imprévu. J'y passe des heures et mon esprit s'y use" (My book is a construction, and there resides what I consider to be my essential work, the most delicate work, moreover. One must link each part to the preceding part, announce what is to come while preserving an effect of surprise. I spend hours on it and wear out my mind with it) (98).

6. These titles were not yet announced with the November 1918 publication of *À l'Ombre des jeunes filles en fleurs* (which appeared in bookstores only in June 1919). Instead, the story of Albertine constituted simple chapters of what Proust then called *Sodome et Gomorrhe II.* See Jean-Yves Tadié's "Introduction générale" to the 1987–89 Pléiade edition (*RTP,* 1:ix-cvii, and in particular lxxxviii-xci).

7. Milly refers to the text's "dysfunction" in *Proust dans le texte et l'avant-texte.* He is speaking of Proust's continual displacement and reconstruction of passages and narrative sequences in *La Prisonnière,* which create a "puzzle without a model" (131).

8. Ellison rightly finds in Feuillerat's study "a powerful intuitive prefiguration of the deepest theoretical considerations now at the forefront of critical attention" (*The Reading of Proust,* 108).

9. On the implications of Feuillerat's argument for queer theory, see my essay "Genetic Aberrations."

10. "Genèse de *Swann*" first appeared in the January 15, 1937, issue of the *Revue d'histoire de la philosophie et d'histoire générale de la civilisation* (5:67–115). On the career of Vigneron's sex-transposition theory, which was widely disseminated in the 1940s through Justin O'Brien's *PMLA* essay "Albertine the Ambiguous," see Ladenson, *Proust's Lesbianism* (13–18).

11. "Désintégration de Marcel Proust" was presented to the Romance Club of the University of Chicago in May 1948 and was first published in *Les Annales de la Faculté des Lettres de Toulouse* in 1960.

12. See Fraisse, "Méthode de composition," 35–82. Apart from Séailles's *Le Génie dans l'art* (1883), Fraisse cites Paul Souriau's *Théorie de l'invention* (1881), Théodule Ribot's *Essai sur l'imagination créatrice* (1900), François Paulhan's *Psychologie de l'invention* (1901), and Henri Bergson's essay "L'Effort intellectuel" (1902). *Le Génie dans l'art* was reissued by Alcan at the height of the trend, in 1897.

13. On the late nineteenth-century surge of interest in vitalistic organicism across the disciplines, see Phillips, "Organicism."

14. Ribot was the author of the trilogy *Les Maladies de la mémoire* (1881), *Les Maladies de la volonté* (1883), and *Les Maladies de la personnalité* (1885), which inventoried and categorized the "pathological" forms of memory, will, and personality. For an excellent discussion of the role of Ribot's work within the nineteenth-century intellectual context of the *Recherche*, see Finn, *Proust, the Body and Literary Form*.

15. When Kolb wrote about Albertine's death in *Lettres retrouvées* (1966), he obviously was not referring to the modified version of her death in Grasset's edition of *Albertine disparue* (1987). In Kolb's preface, the title *Albertine disparue* refers to the volume published as either *Albertine disparue* or *La Fugitive* over the years (notably, *La Fugitive* was adopted by the 1954 Pléiade edition, which explains its widespread referential use from the 1950s to the 1980s).

16. On the genesis of the "roman d'Albertine," see Pugh, *The Growth of À la recherche du temps perdu* (2:735–69), and Mauriac Dyer, *Proust inachevé* (34–37).

17. Here and in Chapter 4, I use the term *intention* in two strictly limited senses. According to the first, references to Proust's "intention[s]" denote instances of specific compositional choices or precise, articulated desires as to the formal appearance of the text. In a second formulation (Chapter 4), the term *final intentions* is used in its technical sense as defined within the field of textual criticism; see McGann, *A Critique of Modern Textual Criticism*.

18. Moreover, Bardèche makes clear reference to their widely disseminated view that the novel was riddled with deforming excrescences. Citing Proust's use of the word *episode* to designate the Albertine narrative,

he adds: "Le plan de toute la *Recherche du temps perdu* devient, en effet, beaucoup plus simple si l'histoire d'Albertine n'est qu'un 'épisode' comme l'était déjà 'Un Amour de Swann.' Car les parties de la *Recherche* se dégagent alors très clairement. . . . Le plan de l'œuvre de Proust, au lieu d'être complexe, sinueux, *engorgé par d'énormes excroissances,* redevient un plan rationnel qui correspond bien au sens que Proust voulait donner à son livre" (The outline of the entire *Recherche du temps perdu* becomes, in effect, much simpler if the story of Albertine is only an "episode" like "Un Amour de Swann" before it. For the parts of the *Recherche* become clear and distinct. . . . The outline of Proust's work, instead of being complex, sinuous, *engorged with enormous excrescences,* would then become a rational plan again, a plan that would correspond perfectly to the meaning Proust wanted to lend his novel) (2:211–12, italics mine).

19. The term *élan vital* (vital impetus) was popularized by Henri Bergson's *Évolution créatrice* (1907). Bergson hypothesized that because all forms of life were the continuation of a single originary impulse (*élan*), "on devrait retrouver, jusque dans les derniers ruisselets, quelque chose de l'impulsion reçue à la source" (one should find, even down to the tiniest rivulets, something of the impetus received at the source) (69).

20. For an insightful dicussion of how the Montjouvain passage functions within a narrative whose comprehension is based on rereading, see Ladenson's "Rereading Proust."

Chapter 4: Grasset's Revenge

1. See Chapter 3, note 17, on my use of the word *intention.*

2. On the tea-stained envelope bearing Proust's last references to the novel, see Mauriac Dyer ("Sur une enveloppe"). Several critics have commented on a *Nota Bene,* crossed out and perhaps interrupted, scrawled by Proust on the typescript and apparently indicating a hesitation as to the organization of the final volumes: "Décidément, non. *La Prisonnière* fera un tout et Albertine" (Definitely not. *La Prisonnière* will be a whole and Albertine). Finally, it is Milly who analyzes the quality of Proust's handwriting in the incipit to *Albertine disparue,* in order to demonstrate that the title predated Proust's extensive revisions ("Retitrage," 148).

3. See Robert Proust's correspondence with the Nouvelle Revue Française, *Les Années perdues de la* Recherche: *1922–31.*

4. Absent from *Albertine disparue* is a key scene that prepares the novel's culminating point in *Le Temps retrouvé,* the hero-narrator's assumption of his literary vocation. The turn to literature is set in motion by a final involuntary memory sequence that begins in the courtyard of the Guermantes mansion. The first involuntary memory refers back to the hero's visit to Saint Mark's baptistry in Venice, where he stood upon two uneven paving-stones—a moment eliminated from *Albertine disparue,*

where the Venice episode is based on an earlier excerpt published in the journal *Feuillets d'Art* ("À Venise").

5. Benjamin identifies the "aura" of a work of art with the authority of the original, whose unique historical existence is bounded by its unreproducible "presence in time and space." "The Work of Art," 222.

6. The *Œuvres libres* hypothesis was first advanced by Pierre-Edmond Robert ("L'Édition des posthumes d'*À la recherche du pemps perdu*") and Haruhiko Tokuda ("Autour d'*Albertine disparue*"), then developed and disseminated by Giovanni Macchia in the Italian newspaper *Corriere della sera* ("Proust: Eccovi il romanzo d'Albertine," October 13, 1991, and "Come perdere e trovare un testo di Proust," October 14, 1991). A French translation of Macchia's two-part article appeared in *La Revue des Lettres modernes, Marcel Proust I* (1992): 127–41 ("Le Roman d'Albertine"). See Mauriac Dyer's most recent rejection of this hypothesis in *Proust inachevé* (117–24).

7. See Beretta Anguissola, "Le Doute philologique." The hypothesis is developed at length in Beretta Anguissola's introduction to *Albertine scomparsa*, "La 'querelle' di 'Albertine scomparsa'" (*Alla ricerca del tempo perduto*, 4:782–97). Milly's positions are best summarized in his "Problèmes génétiques."

8. Mauriac Dyer refers to the Pléiade's restoration of the text as an effort to restitute to the double its *physionomie d'origine* ("Mirages," 121). Starobinski has similarly defined the object of traditional textual criticism as the effort to uncover a text's *visage authentique* (authentic face)— "comme on nettoie les peintures enfumées et surchargées" (just as one cleans paintings blackened with the layers of time). "La Littérature," 170.

9. Milly's *Albertine disparue*, which now replaces *La Fugitive* as the sixth volume of Flammarion's *À la recherche du temps perdu*, took over ten years to get there: it was first published separately by Slatkine only after Flammarion refused to integrate it into the *Recherche*. Milly, "De l'art de conférer," 82, n. 1.

10. In the information age, the word *deletion* has taken on the sense of an immediate erasure. But as the *Oxford English Dictionary* indicates, "to delete" also has a more attenuated meaning: "To strike or blot out . . . (written or printed characters)." I speak of deletions here to describe instances in which Proust marked passages for omission—even if that omission was meant to be temporary. English offers no equivalent to the French verb *supprimer* or to its corresponding substantive, *suppression*, which tend to signify removal (of written material) rather than erasure.

11. See Mauriac Dyer's fascinating chapter "Horizons intentionnels du texte inachevé," in *Proust inachevé* (171–209).

12. I am borrowing these terms, tongue in cheek, from Starobinski's *Jean-Jacques Rousseau: La Transparence et l'obstacle* (1957). The terms take on an interesting new resonance in the context of posthumous editing.

13. I speak of an editorial process with respect to the work of Grasset and Gallimard, even though the two men fulfilled the functions of publisher rather than editor. The kinds of decisions they made with respect to the form of the text, quite apart from their responsibility for publicity and distribution, make the assimilation possible. The French word *éditeur*, of course, makes no distinction between the two.

14. Proust's footnote to his translation of John Ruskin's *Sesame and Lilies*: *Sésame et les lys*, 134–36, n. 24.

15. Compagnon's *Proust Between Two Centuries* situates Proust's novel between these two alternatives. "Proust cannot exhaust the problem of the unity of the work," Compagnon concludes. "If the novels of the nineteenth century are incomplete because their unity is retrospective and in that sense fortuitous, and if a preconceived unity remains dogmatic and artificial, what will be the unity of the greatest work of the in-between time of the centuries, perhaps even of the twentieth century? It would have to be both . . . organic and formal, vital and at the same time logical" (40).

16. "Les Nouvelles Éditions," 144. The Livre de Poche Classique edition presents the text of *Albertine disparue* before that of *La Fugitive*, whose composition, as Milly notes, preceded it.

17. Although Feuillerat's theory of the two Prousts has been debunked, many of his conclusions regarding the evolution of *À la recherche du temps perdu* remain pertinent. His commentary on the thematic character of Proust's additions to the Albertine narrative, with their concentration on doubt and suspicion, is corroborated by more recent genetic criticism. See Compagnon, "Notice" to *Sodome et Gomorrhe, RTP* 3: 1185–1261, and Pugh, *The Growth of* À la recherche du temps perdu, 2:755–56.

18. For an excellent discussion of the centrality of this obsession to the novel as a whole, see Ladenson, *Proust's Lesbianism*.

19. McGinnis makes the same point as to the interpretive nature of the new *dénouement*, but he emphasizes that for once the narrator's conclusions are not overturned and can thus be considered definitive ("L'Inconnaissable Gomorrhe," 101).

20. The foreshortening of mourning also eliminates, of course, interesting interpretive possibilities, such as Ricciardi's fascinating chapter on Proust in her book *The Ends of Mourning*—an analysis based in part on a reading of mourning in *La Fugitive* (69–119).

21. See Milly, "L'Accueil d'*Albertine disparue*."

22. The edition of *Jean Santeuil* followed a similar path. When Pierre Clarac published his version of *Jean Santeuil* in 1971, he presented it as a deconstruction of the first edition: "En 1954, M. Bernard de Fallois a donné une première édition de *Jean Santeuil*, en trois volumes. Il y combinait . . . les fragments de cette œuvre interrompue, pour essayer de la présenter comme un roman bien construit. Nous pensions, Ferré et moi, qu'un jour il faudrait la faire connaître dans l'état d'inachèvement où

Proust l'a laissée" (In 1954, Bernard de Fallois gave us the first edition of *Jean Santeuil*, in three volumes. There he combined . . . the fragments of this interrupted work, in order to present it as a well-constructed novel. Ferré and I thought that one day it should be made available in its unfinished state, such as Proust left it) ("Avant-propos," *Jean Santeuil*, ix).

23. Gallimard did, however, publish a somewhat revised edition of *Albertine disparue* in response to Mauriac Dyer's critique. The updated edition, *Albertine Disparue* [*The Fugitive*], edited by Anne Chevalier, appeared in Gallimard's Collection Folio and its Collection Blanche (1992) and then in the Bibliothèque de la Pléiade (1994).

Epilogue

1. See Brooks, "The Shape of Time." Brooks specifies that "American copyright law allowed Random House to renew its copyright on the last three parts of Scott Moncrieff-Kilmartin-Enright: 'The Prisoner,' 'The Fugitive' and 'Time Regained.'"

2. This criticism was at the heart of Shattuck's well-publicized proposal to boycott the 1987–89 Pléiade edition: "Every time we cite the new Pléiade edition, we are endorsing a scholarly enterprise that seeks not to identify and present the text of a major literary work but to blur and smear it back into a congeries of manuscripts" ("Looking Backward," 10). The new Pléiade has, of course, now superseded its 1954 predecessor as the edition of reference for scholars.

WORKS CITED

Adorno, Theodor. "Bibliographical Musings." In *Notes to Literature*. Vol. 2. Trans. Shierry Weber Nicholsen. New York: Columbia University Press, 1991. 20–31.

Alden, Douglas. *Marcel Proust's Grasset Proofs*. Chapel Hill: University of North Carolina Press, 1978.

Aristotle. *Poetics*. Trans. Malcolm Heath. London: Penguin Books, 1996.

Assouline, Pierre. *Gaston Gallimard*. Paris: Balland, 1984.

Bardèche, Maurice. *Marcel Proust romancier*. 2 vols. Paris: Les Sept Couleurs, 1971.

Bayard, Pierre. *Le Hors-sujet: Proust et la digression*. Paris: Minuit, 1996.

Benjamin, Walter. "The Work of Art in the Age of Mechanical Reproduction." In *Illuminations*. Ed. Hannah Arendt. Trans. Harry Zohn. New York: Harcourt, Brace and World, 1968. 219–53.

Beretta Anguissola, Alberto. "Le Doute philologique." *Bulletin d'informations proustiennes* 29 (1998): 67–80.

Bergson, Henri. *Évolution créatrice*. Geneva: Skira, 1945 [1907].

Bersani, Leo. *Marcel Proust: The Fictions of Life and of Art*. New York: Oxford University Press, 1965.

Boillat, Gabriel. *La Librairie Bernard Grasset et les lettres françaises*. Paris: Champion, 1974.

Bonnet, Henri. "La Publication de *Du côté de chez Swann*." In *Marcel Proust de 1907 à 1914*. Vol. 2. Paris: Nizet, 1976. 119–25.

Bourget, Paul. *Essais de psychologie contemporaine*. Paris: Lemerre, 1883.

Bowie, Malcolm. *Freud, Proust and Lacan: Theory as Fiction*. Cambridge: Cambridge University Press, 1987.

Brooks, Peter. *Body Work: Objects of Desire in Modern Narrative*. Cambridge, Mass.: Harvard University Press, 1993.

———. "The Shape of Time." *The New York Times Book Review*, January 25, 2004, 11.

Bürger, Peter. *Theory of the Avant-Garde*. Trans. Michael Shaw. Minneapolis: University of Minnesota Press, 1984.

Cano, Christine M. "Genetic Aberrations: The Two Faces of Proust." *Textual Practice* 17, no. 1 (Spring 2003): 41–60.

———. "Mea Culpa: Gide, Proust, and the Nouvelle Revue Française." *Romance Quarterly* 50, no. 1 (Winter 2003): 33–42.

Carter, William C. *Marcel Proust: A Life*. New Haven and London: Yale University Press, 2000.

Compagnon, Antoine. "Ce qu'on ne peut plus dire de Proust." *Littérature* 88 (December 1992): 54–61.

———. *Proust entre deux siècles*. Paris: Seuil, 1989. English trans.: *Proust Between Two Centuries*. Trans. Richard E. Goodkin. New York: Columbia University Press, 1992.

De Man, Paul. "Reading (Proust)." In *Allegories of Reading*. New Haven and London: Yale University Press, 1979. 57–78.

Dezon-Jones, Elyane. "Éditer Proust: hier, aujourd'hui et peut-être demain." *Littérature* 88 (December 1992): 46–53.

Dreyfus, Robert. *Souvenirs sur Marcel Proust*. Paris: Grasset, 1926.

Dubois, Jacques. *Pour Albertine: Proust et le sens du social*. Paris: Seuil, 1997.

Ellison, David. *The Reading of Proust*. Baltimore: Johns Hopkins University Press, 1984.

Faÿ, Bernard. *Les Précieux*. Paris: Librairie Académique Perrin, 1966.

Feuillerat, Albert. *Comment Marcel Proust a composé son roman*. New Haven and London: Yale University Press, 1934.

Finn, Michael R. *Proust, the Body and Literary Form*. Cambridge: Cambridge University Press, 1999.

Fraisse, Luc. *Lire Du côté de chez Swann*. Paris: Dunod, 1993.

———. "Méthode de composition: Marcel Proust lecteur d'Edgar Poe." In *Marcel Proust 1. À la recherche du temps perdu: Des personnages aux structures*. Paris-Caen: Les Lettres Modernes Minard, 1992. 35–82.

Freud, Sigmund. *The Interpretation of Dreams*. Trans. A. A. Brill. New York: Macmillan, 1937. 269–72.

Genette, Gérard. *Figures III*. Paris: Seuil, 1972.

Gray, Margaret. *Postmodern Proust*. Philadelphia: University of Pennsylvania Press, 1992.

Hayman, Ronald. *Proust: A Biography*. London: Minerva, 1990.

Henry, Anne. *Marcel Proust: Théories pour une esthétique*. Paris: Klincksieck, 1981.

———. *Proust romancier: Le Tombeau égyptien*. Paris: Flammarion, 1983.

Ippolito, Marguerite-Marie. "À la recherche du temps protégé." In *Le Magazine Littéraire* 246 (October 1987): 32–33.

Jakobson, Roman, and Morris Hale. *Fundamentals of Language*. 'S Gravenhage: Mouton and Co., 1956.

Jenny, Laurent. "Genetic Criticism and Its Myths." *Yale French Studies* 89 (1996): 9–25.

Kolb, Philip. "Inadvertent Repetitions of Material in *À la recherche du temps perdu*." *PMLA* 51 (1936): 249–62.

Krieger, Murray. *A Reopening of Closure: Organicism Against Itself*. New York: Columbia University Press, 1989.

———. "The 'Imaginary' and Its Enemies." *New Literary History* 31, no. 1 (Winter 2000): 129–62.

Kristeva, Julia. *Le Temps sensible: Proust et l'expérience littéraire.* Paris: Gallimard, 1994. English trans.: *Time and Sense: Proust and the Experience of Literature.* Trans. Ross Guberman. New York: Columbia University Press, 1996.

Lacan, Jacques. "L'Instance de la lettre dans l'inconscient." In *Écrits.* Vol. 1. Paris: Seuil, 1966.

Ladenson, Elisabeth. *Proust's Lesbianism.* Ithaca and London: Cornell University Press, 1999.

———. "Rereading Proust: Perversion and Prolepsis in *À la recherche du temps perdu.*" In *Second Thoughts: A Focus on Rereading.* Ed. David Galef. Detroit: Wayne State University Press, 1998. 249–65.

Lhomeau, Franck, and Alain Coelho. *Marcel Proust à la recherche d'un éditeur.* Paris: Orban, 1988.

Macchia, Giovanni. *L'Ange de la nuit.* Trans. Paul Bédarida, Mario Fusco, and Marie-France Merger. Paris: Gallimard, 1993.

Mauriac Dyer, Nathalie. "*Albertine disparue, Les Œuvres libres,* et l'oubli." Bulletin d'informations proustiennes 29 (1998): 85–101.

———. "Le Cycle de *Sodome et Gomorrhe:* remarques sur la tomaison d'*À la recherche du temps perdu.*" *Littérature* 88 (December 1992): 62–71.

———. "Les Mirages du double: *Albertine disparue* selon la Pléiade (1989)." *Bulletin Marcel Proust* 40 (1990): 117–53.

———. *Proust inachevé. Le dossier "Albertine disparue."* Paris: Champion, 2005.

———. "Proust procruste: les fins disjointes d'*À la recherche du temps perdu.*" *Marcel Proust 3. Nouvelles directions de la recherche proustienne 2.* Paris-Caen: Les Lettres Modernes Minard (2001): 129–44.

———. "Sur une enveloppe souillée de tisane: un plan pour la suite d'*Albertine disparue.*" *Bulletin Marcel Proust* 42 (1992): 19–25.

Maurois, André. *À la recherche de Marcel Proust.* Paris: Hachette, 1949. English trans.: *Proust: Portrait of a Genius.* Trans. Gerard Hopkins. New York: Harper and Brothers, 1950.

McDonald, Christie. *The Proustian Fabric: Associations of Memory.* Lincoln: University of Nebraska Press, 1992.

McGann, Jerome. *A Critique of Modern Textual Criticism.* Chicago: University of Chicago Press, 1983.

McGinnis, Reginald. "L'Inconnaissable Gomorrhe: à propos d'*Albertine disparue.*" *Romanic Review* 81, no. 1 (January 1990): 92–104.

Milly, Jean. "L'Accueil d'*Albertine disparue* par la critique en 1926." *Bulletin de la Société des Amis de Marcel Proust* 35 (1985): 326–37.

———. "De l'art de conférer (réponse à Alberto Beretta Anguissola)." *Bulletin d'informations proustiennes* 29 (1998): 81–83.

———. "Faut-il changer la fin du roman de Proust?" *Études françaises* 30, no. 1 (Summer 1994): 15–32.

———. "Les Nouvelles Éditions des parties posthumes d'*À la recherche du temps perdu*." *Bulletin Marcel Proust* 44 (1994): 141–48.

———. "Problèmes génétiques et éditoriaux à propos d'*Albertine disparue*." In *Marcel Proust, écrire sans fin*. Ed. Jean Milly and Rainer Warning. Paris: CNRS Editions, 1996. 51–77.

———. *Proust dans le texte et l'avant-texte*. Paris: Flammarion, 1985.

———. "Retitrage, recyclage et autres visages d'*Albertine disparue*." *Bulletin Marcel Proust* 41 (1991): 147–56.

Müller, Günther. "Erzählzeit und erzählte Zeit." In *Morphologische Poetik*. Ed. Elena Müller. Tübingen: Max Niemeyer, 1968. 269–86.

O'Brien, Justin. "Albertine the Ambiguous: Notes on Proust's Transposition of Sexes." *PMLA* 64 (1949): 933–52.

Painter, George D. *Marcel Proust*. 2 vols. London: Chatto and Windus, 1965.

Parinet, Elisabeth. "L'Édition littéraire, 1890–1914." In *L'Histoire de l'édition française: Le Livre concurrencé, 1900–1950*. Vol. 4. Ed. Roger Chartier, Henri-Jean Martin, and Jean-Pierre Vivet. Paris: Promodis, 1986. 148–87.

Paulhan, François. *Psychologie de l'invention*. Paris: Alcan, 1930 [1901].

Phillips, D. C. "Organicism in the Late Nineteenth and Early Twentieth Centuries." *Journal of the History of Ideas* 31 (July–September 1970): 413–32.

Pierre-Quint, Léon. *Proust et la stratégie littéraire*. Paris: Corrêa, 1954. First published as *Comment parut Du côté de chez Swann*. Paris: Kra, 1930.

Poulet, Georges. *L'Espace proustien*. Paris: Gallimard, 1963. English trans.: *Proustian Space*. Trans. Elliott Coleman. Baltimore and London: Johns Hopkins University Press, 1977.

Proust, Marcel. *À la recherche du temps perdu*. 4 vols. Bibliothèque de la Pléiade. Paris: Gallimard, 1987–89.

———. *Albertine disparue*. Ed. Nathalie Mauriac and Étienne Wolff. Paris: Grasset, 1987.

———. *Albertine disparue*. Ed. Jean Milly. Paris: Flammarion, 2003.

———. *Alla ricerca del tempo perduto*. 4 vols. Trans. Giovanni Raboni. Milan: Mondadori, 1993.

———. *À un ami*. Ed. Georges de Lauris. Paris: Amiot-Dumont, 1948.

———. "À Venise." *Feuillets d'Art* 4 (December 15, 1919): 1–12.

———. *Le Carnet de 1908*. Ed. Philip Kolb. Paris: Gallimard, 1978.

———. *Correspondance*. 21 vols. Ed. Philip Kolb. Paris: Plon, 1970–93.

———, and Gaston Gallimard. *Correspondance*. Ed. Pascal Fouché. Paris: Gallimard, 1989.

———. *Jean Santeuil*, preceded by *Les Plaisirs et les jours*. Ed. Pierre Clarac and Yves Sandre. Bibliothèque de la Pléiade. Paris: Gallimard, 1971.

———. *Lettres retrouvées.* Ed. Philip Kolb. Paris: Plon, 1966.

———. *Remembrance of Things Past.* Trans. C. K. Scott Moncrieff, Terence Kilmartin, and Andreas Mayor. 3 vols. New York: Random House, 1981.

———. *Selected Letters.* Ed. Philip Kolb. Trans. Terence Kilmartin, Joanna Kilmartin, and Ralph Manheim. 4 vols. Various publishers, 1983–2000.

Proust, Robert, and the Nouvelle Revue Française. *Les Années perdues de la Recherche: 1922–1931.* Ed. Nathalie Mauriac-Dyer. Paris: Gallimard, 1999.

Pugh, Anthony R. *The Birth of* À la recherche du temps perdu. Lexington: French Forum, 1987.

———. "The Ending of *Swann* Revisited." *Modern Philology* 99, no. 3 (2002): 357–75.

———. *The Growth of* À la recherche du temps perdu: *A Chronological Examination of Proust's Manuscripts from 1909 to 1914.* 2 vols. Toronto: University of Toronto Press, 2004.

Raimond, Michel, and Luc Fraisse. *Proust en toutes lettres.* Paris: Bordas, 1989.

Ribot, Théodule. *Essai sur l'imagination créatrice.* Paris: Alcan, 1900.

Ricciardi, Alessia. *The Ends of Mourning: Psychoanalysis, Literature, Film.* Stanford: Stanford University Press, 2003.

Ricœur, Paul. *Temps et récit II.* Paris: Seuil, 1984.

Robert, Louis de. *Comment débuta Marcel Proust.* Paris: Gallimard, 1969.

Robert, Pierre-Edmond. "L'Édition des posthumes d'*À la recherche du temps perdu.*" *Bulletin de la Société des Amis de Marcel Proust* 38 (1988): 95–101.

Rousset, Jean. *Forme et signification.* Paris: Corti, 1962.

Ruskin, John. *Sésame et les lys.* Trans. Marcel Proust. Ed. Antoine Compagnon. Brussels: Complexe, 1987.

Shattuck, Roger. "Looking Backward: Genetic Criticism and the Genetic Fallacy." In *Origins and Identities in French Literature* [French Literature Series 26]. Ed. Buford Norman. Amsterdam and Atlanta: Rodopi, 1999. 1–14.

———. *Proust's Way: A Field Guide to* In Search of Lost Time. New York: W. W. Norton and Company, 2000.

Séailles, Gabriel. *Le Génie dans l'art.* Paris: Alcan, 1923 [1883].

Souriau, Paul. *Théorie de l'invention.* Paris: Hachette, 1881.

Spitzer, Leo. "Le style de Marcel Proust." In *Études de style.* Trans. Eliane Kaufholz, Alain Coulon, and Michel Foucault. Paris: Gallimard, 1970. 397–473. First published in *Stilstudien.* Munich: Max Hueber, 1961.

Starobinski, Jean. *Jean-Jacques Rousseau: La Transparence et l'obstacle.* Paris: Plon, 1957.

———. "La Littérature: Le Texte et l'interprète." In *Faire de l'histoire: Nouvelles approches.* Vol. 2. Ed. Jacques Le Goff and Pierre Nora. Paris: Gallimard, 1974. 168–82.

Tadié, Jean-Yves. *Marcel Proust.* Paris: Gallimard, 1996. English trans.: *Marcel Proust.* Trans. Euan Cameron. New York: Viking Penguin, 2000.

——. *Proust et le roman.* Paris: Gallimard, 1971.

Tokuda, Haruhiko. "Autour d'*Albertine disparue.*" *Études de sciences humaines* 90 (March 1991): 181–94.

Vigneron, Robert. "Désintégration de Marcel Proust." In *Études sur Stendhal et sur Proust.* Paris: Nizet, 1978. 501–32.

——. "Genèse de *Swann.*" In *Études sur Stendhal et sur Proust.* 308–51.

Winton, Alison. *Proust's Additions: The Making of* À la recherche du temps perdu. 2 vols. Cambridge: Cambridge University Press, 1977.

INDEX

CHRISTINE M. CANO is an associate professor of French and comparative literature at Case Western Reserve University in Cleveland, Ohio.

*The University of Illinois Press
is a founding member of the
Association of American University Presses.*

---

*Composed in 9.5/12.5 Trump Mediaeval
with Trump Mediaeval display
by BookComp, Inc.
Manufactured by Maple-Vail
Book Manufacturing Group*

*University of Illinois Press
1325 South Oak Street
Champaign, IL 61820-6903
www.press.uillinois.edu*